Native American Autobiography
Redefined

PETER LANG
New York • Washington, D.C./Baltimore • Bern
Frankfurt am Main • Berlin • Brussels • Vienna • Oxford

Stephanie A. Sellers

Native American Autobiography Redefined

A HANDBOOK

PETER LANG
New York • Washington, D.C./Baltimore • Bern
Frankfurt am Main • Berlin • Brussels • Vienna • Oxford

Library of Congress Cataloging-in-Publication Data

Sellers, Stephanie A.
Native American autobiography redefined: a handbook / Stephanie A. Sellers.
p. cm.
Includes bibliographical references.
1. Indian women—North America—Biography. 2. Autobiography—Authorship.
3. Brant, Molly, 1736–1796. 4. Mohawk women—Biography.
5. Feminist literary criticism. I. Title.
E89.S14   973.04'97'00922—dc22   2005012817
ISBN-13: 978-0-8204-7944-6
ISBN-10: 0-8204-7944-6

Bibliographic information published by **Die Deutsche Bibliothek**.
Die Deutsche Bibliothek lists this publication in the "Deutsche
Nationalbibliografie"; detailed bibliographic data is available
on the Internet at http://dnb.ddb.de/.

Cover design by Joni Holst

The paper in this book meets the guidelines for permanence and durability
of the Committee on Production Guidelines for Book Longevity
of the Council of Library Resources.

© 2007 Peter Lang Publishing, Inc., New York
29 Broadway, 18th floor, New York, NY 10006
www.peterlang.com

Printed in the United States of America

❈ TABLE OF CONTENTS

 Preface

Interest in books about the Indians, or Native North Americans, continues to grow in the United States and Europe. As our world society becomes increasingly modernized, meaning less connected to the natural world and noticing less our spiritual connection to each other, it only makes sense that the inhabitants of Turtle Island (North America) turn to the ancient cultures of this land: the cultures of the First Nations peoples. Regardless of one's ethnicity, race, or religious beliefs, Americans need the wisdom of the elder Native nations and their teachings of peace and balanced living more than ever. We must also ask this: What do the Native nations need from the larger American culture both within and outside institutions of higher learning? They need cultural recognition, respect, rights, and peace. Some say that the Smithsonian Museum of the American Indian in Washington, D.C., was an important beginning in gaining those values. I believe there is also another way: through the books that, despite the popularity of the Internet, human beings still value and learn from. Through an educated population, cultural recognition, and rights for Native nations will grow. Education is always the key to ending the ignorance that creates and perpetuates oppression and injustice.

Colonization of Native peoples along with religious, school, and government policies against them was and still is supported and perpetuated by the written word. Both academic texts and books for the common person aid/ed and abet/ed colonization as well. What was used to disperse and destroy culture must now be used to gather and grow that culture: return it to wholeness on the page and therefore in the minds of the people. This goal can be achieved by allowing Native culture to be expressed via, within, and through the written word and create a shape for those words that is undeniably indigenous. The biographies of some Native elders have been used to perpetuate negative, flawed images of Native peoples. We must now use both the content and the popularity of these biographies to reverse this damage.

Promoting the sociopolitical empowerment of Native American peoples and improving the education of the general citizenry of the United States about Native American peoples, culture, and history is a primary goal in revising present works in the Native American Autobiography genre, and in creating more works that are defined as Indigenous Communal Narrative. I envision this happening through additions to, revisions of, and further elaboration—perhaps entire new re-creations—on works of Native American Autobiography. This genre is a superior tool to teach the non-Native population, the general readership of the United States—or any country—about Native people. However, the achievement of this goal is absolutely contingent upon these criteria: The work must demonstrate Native methodology, present a rendering of history that is Native-centered, and offer an unbiased presentation of perceptions of Native women. Mohawk poet Maurice Kenny and scholars Paula Gunn Allen and Jay Miller have all accomplished the task and offer superb models of Indigenous Communal Narrative for others in this field to emulate.

The audience for these works is not only students and faculty of the academy. Indeed, they are for a much larger community: Native American peoples, Native American scholars specifically and any scholar interested in this subject in general, the general United States population, and the academic and nonacademic world community. Therefore, to frame my work solely for an academic audience would disregard some of the very people and communities it is intended to benefit. How this work benefits these communities is by offering further examination of a still predominantly hidden literary genre that when further examined, only tends to obscure or distort its subject: Native American peoples and history. This is a problem not only for indigenous peoples worldwide, but for all peoples worldwide.

In the Introduction of her work titled *Pocahontas: Medicine Woman, Spy, Entrepreneur, Diplomat* (2003), Paula Gunn Allen makes these observations:

> The modern way to write a biography involves, among other things, a process that singles out an individual, cuts her out of the total biota or life system

within which she lives and from which she derives her identity, gives her value and prestige *above* the rest. But in Native traditional life stories, the subject of the biography—or, often autobiography—is situated within the entire life system: that community of living things, geography, climate, spirit, people, and supernaturals ...(2)

What I wish to contribute to the ongoing discussion about Native American Autobiography is to encourage what Paula Gunn Allen refers to as "the narrative tradition of a community." This concept embodies the description of Native methodology in regards to recreating an autobiography of a Native American to educate the general population. Students in institutions of higher learning and scholars should of course make use of all the materials available to them, including the broader discussion about this genre. They are, however, a small percentage of the United States population, and I do not believe they hold the answer to entirely reversing our present state of ignorance of things Native American. Measures must be directed toward the general United States population to reverse and heal the acute damage inflicted upon Native people and their cultures for the past 500 years; the empowerment of Native peoples accompanies the re-education of the American public. This process of revealing cultural experience and identity through writing and literary study blossomed in North America in the 1960s and 1970s as many silenced and oppressed groups began to socially come forward through their written words. Moving out of the age of ethnographic autobiography and into one of communal narrative is another beginning for Native American communities. Herein is the purpose of redefining the genre with Native cultural perspective. Literary scholars cannot simply continue examining these texts as literary artifacts, but must make them into something they should have been from the beginning: a way for non-Native peoples to know and appreciate Native peoples and their nations as they truly were/are.

My hope is that scholars and writers interested in this field will pick up the Native American autobiographies of the past and rework them into the powerful teaching tools they can become. Second, my immediate intention is that the readers of the most popular autobiographies, like *Black Elk Speaks*, will become informed ones and learn to spot western culture standing in for Native culture. I also hope we will see in America and throughout the world more books qualified to be Indigenous Communal Narratives so our world community might come to learn much more comprehensively and accurately about the magnificent cultures of the indigenous nations.

I write these words a mere twenty miles from Carlisle, Pennsylvania, where the infamous Carlisle Indian School, now the site of the United States Army War College, still stands as a beacon of Native North American ethnic cleansing and cultural silencing. Though we can no longer see the piles of hacked off braids and the discarded moccasins, blankets, and clothing of indigenous children, the spirits of these truths still roam and trouble the living. We must evoke the voices of our Native ancestors through the vehicle of indigenous cultural knowledge expressed in the format of Indigenous Communal Narratives and allow what has been silenced to speak at last. It is not sufficient for only the Native people to remember the losses of the past, as they do, but we must collectively remember as a nation for that is how we need to be healed.

Stephanie A. Sellers
Gettysburg, Pennsylvania

ACKNOWLEDGMENTS

I would like to express my gratitude to several people who helped me during the research and writing process. Among the elder colleagues to whom I am most deeply grateful are Paula Gunn Allen and Barbara Alice Mann who guided and encouraged me in the original concept and throughout the writing of this book. I am humbly indebted to them and their cumulative decades of researching and writing that makes the work of those from my generation much more manageable. I wish to also thank Elizabeth Minnich for reading and offering lengthy comments on one of the first drafts of the manuscript.

I am also grateful to Heidi Burns, senior editor at Peter Lang, who offered important suggestions for revisions and much patient and generous encouragement.

Finally, the help I received from Kim Breighner of Gettysburg College in making my manuscript camera ready was invaluable, and I am especially thankful for her expertise.

Grateful acknowledgment is hereby made to copyright holders for permission to use the following copyrighted material:

Maurice Kenny, *Tekonwatonti/Molly Brant: Poems of War*, 1981. Used by permission of White Pine Press.

CHAPTER ONE

Native American Autobiography Reexamined

There are three types of autobiography: the literary genre brought by the Europeans during colonization of North America and the genre Arnold Krupat named Native American autobiography in the 1980s. What has emerged from many sources over the past few decades is the term *communal narrative*: a literary genre I refer to as Indigenous Communal Narrative. This genre more accurately describes what should be presented as a book about an individual indigenous person, rather than the Native American autobiographical works created by EuroAmericans before and shortly after the year 1900. What has come before the modern day written communal narratives (such as Paula Gunn Allen's work on Pocahontas, Jay Miller's text about Mourning Dove, and Maurice Kenny's poetry collection on Tekonwatonti) are highly biased pieces of writing about Native people (primarily males) that distort Native history, Native culture, and thus the cumulative Native legacy and future. The as-told-to books by ethnographers of the past that Krupat categorized as Native American autobiographies present specific problems. One of the most famous is the book *Black Elk Speaks* by John Neihardt.

Indigenous Communal Narrative is an answer to the problems presented by these books that clarifies literary concepts and representations of Native peoples and cultures, corrects historic and cultural inaccuracies, and serves as a superb teaching tool for future generations of all peoples.

The Native American autobiographies written by ethnographers of the 1700s, 1800s, and early 1900s currently in publication and in most bookstores in America primarily speak for all the Native nations. They are accepted as truth or an accurate rendering of Native American cultural and personal experience. The literary creation called autobiography came to North America with Europeans several hundred years ago during North American colonization. Autobiography is the practice of speaking of the self and of one's notable life experiences in written form. The genre is distinguished from biography in that in autobiography the writer and the subject are one and the same. This literary mode stems from the beliefs and values of European, or western, culture. In that culture the self is the center, the hub from which all experiences are processed, expressed, and understood. Individualism is highly prized and rewarded, and becoming a "dynamic individual" often means social, political, and monetary gain.

In *The Norton Anthology of Literature by Women*, editors Sandra Gilbert and Susan Gubar assert that, "the philosophical foundations of Western literature [and]...the European world view had been based on a hierarchy of the created world which extended from God to man to woman and then to animals, plants, and stones" (6). They note that the western literary canon is built at the onset solely on works by men and these works routinely defamed women (2). Examples they cite include the so-called great Anglo-Saxon epic *Beowulf* from the eighth century and Chaucer's *Canterbury Tales* that was published between 1386 and 1400 (1). The experiences and dramas of the individual are emphasized as most important and characterized in the overall society as paramount components to understanding that culture's history and people. Both the autobiographical literary mode and the cultural beliefs from which it springs are antithetical to the cultures of Native American peoples.

Issues about defining "self" are central to the discussion about autobiography. However, how "self" is transmitted and defined differs between cultures. An individual from a communal people thinks of herself always in terms of the community, not of the "I" in relation to one's group, and indeed, not as an "I" at all but as a "We." In *Native American Speakers of the Eastern Woodlands*, Barbara Mann elaborates on Eastern Woodlands peoples' use of the singular collective pronoun. Consequently, the person may speak using the "I," but will mean the "One" of her or his community (49). The important point for this discussion is that the statement of "I" to a European is a specific reference to the self or to the individual. For the Native American, the "I" or self has no intrinsic meaning separate from the community nation, so that at this foundational point, the literary genres vary dramatically and distinctly from each other. Writing specifically about Arnold Krupat's discussion of Native American autobiography, Lisa J. Udel notes that "western autobiography, celebrating the autonomous individual pitted against and victorious over social and cultural obstacles, is alien to communal-based cultures of native America. The western tradition of a sequential, cumulative narration of a life, as well as the written aspect of autobiography, also conflicted with the traditions of Native America" ("Native American..." 175).

Other ways a Native American text defined as autobiography is distinguished from a European one is the subject's cultural background and what that implies about word choice (as in reference to the self) and origination of the story. Northeastern Native Americans practice oral transmission and are communal people, and these traditions define how stories are told and the role of the storyteller. Both oral transmission and communal thinking are antithetical to the prevailing EuroAmerican culture. This creates serious difficulty when EuroAmericans interview Native Americans for a book or when a EuroAmerican tells the story of a Native American, most especially the story of a Native American woman. This last point is the most challenging of all because of acutely different perceptions of women between EuroAmerican and Native American cultures, particularly the Iroquois.

Native American scholar Paula Gunn Allen offers a list of criteria defining Native American oral literature in the book she edited titled *Studies in American Indian Literature*. She outlines the communal characteristics of Native philosophy as it pertains to literature. They include: cultural knowledge and background of Native American oral literature; it is not about personal expression but brings the isolated self into harmony with communal reality; it redirects the private emotion's energy and integrates it cosmically with the Greater/higher self and universe (all-that-is); and last, Native American literature adds to the medicine wheel (4).

Within this description lies the essence of communal thinking, a defining point in understanding and authentically experiencing Native American literature, especially autobiography. To Native Americans the self is merely part of the whole universe: the nations of people, animals, plants, trees, stars, and so on. A Native person does not distinguish her or himself as an individual, separate from all the other beings and nations of life. Though traditionally there was/is most definitely personal responsibility, personal pride, and endeavors for personal excellence; however, they were all within and for the benefit of community, not to establish oneself as separate or above one's community. Native life philosophy and practices are not divisive (*Seeing with a Native...* 34). Further, the stories themselves are one of those nations, a collective of beings that traditional Keepers transmit and often add their own creative or evaluative spin to the story. The stories are beings: living teachers and holders of history and rich knowing. The Keeper or storyteller, who embodies and holds a position of sacred duty and honor, keeps the stories of her or his nation. She or he looks after them as if they were a treasured grandparent.

Origination of the story is another point of difference between Native and EuroAmerican storytelling. Origination asks, where did the story come from? Does the storyteller create the story, and, if so, does the story belong to the storyteller? In western culture, stories published as books are believed to be created by the author, unless the work is clearly noted as a folk tale or a traditional story. This method applies especially to autobiographies. Often autobiographies are titled "My Story" or "My Life." Readers understand that the story is about the individual, and that the work is entirely singular just as the person's life and her or his experiences are. It is her or his story in the most literal of terms and its purpose is not to demonstrate cultural philosophy and represent one's nation, but to draw attention to and set apart the individual.

To the Native American, stories originate from the great story wheel: from the universe, from the collective storytellers of all times, from the earth and the cosmos. This is not a romanticized, New Age style philosophy concocted out of mismatched slices of so-called Native tradition that bases its premise on stereotypes of Native culture garnered from movies and myths. Indeed, it is not fantasy, or fantastical, at all; but real tradition based in time-honored practices and beliefs that differ from Native nation to Native nation. Stories are for the people in order to keep them well, balanced, and sane as Paula Gunn Allen says in her definition above. As the Native scholar Louis Owens notes, "Native literature [stories] seek transcendence and the recovery of eternal and immutable elements represented by a spiritual tradition that escapes historical fixation" (*Other Destinies*...20). The teller may make her own stylistic changes and adjustments, but the essence of a nation's story remains the same. Barbara Mann notes that, "...sometimes profoundly different Keepings exist concerning the identities, behavior, and deeds of the key individuals of the epoch...[and the] Iroquois have never sought to dictate what people may hear or must believe; hence all versions are traditionally 'correct'" (*Encyclopedia of*...265). Examples she cites that demonstrate the many versions of Keepings of the Great Law include David Cusick's 1825 "Sketches of Ancient History of the Six Nations" that is "one of the oldest written versions of the tradition of the law, as well as in Elias Johnson's 1881 rendition" (266). So the very perception of where the story originates—from either the cosmos (Native) or from the individual (western culture)—dramatically affects the audience's understanding of the story or book.

How Native American communal culture in relation to storytelling and personal testimony is practiced is the third significant literary challenge for EuroAmerican audiences and story gatherers to navigate. One example of this is in the Iroquois culture and how they "operated on the principle of One-Mindedness, or functional consensus, the highest cultural value" Barbara Mann writes in *Iroquoian Women: The Gantowisas* (166). One-Mindedness is achieved by speaking "The Words Before All Else" which is the calling together of all spirits in order to create consensus among all sentient beings (166). EuroAmerican scholars often refer to this practice as the "Thanksgiving Address" before councils (166). These spirits include Mother Earth, animals, plants, waters, the Thunderers, Grandmother Moon, the Milky Way, and so on (166). Mann notes that the "spirit power of important leaders was so strong that the One Mind of their councils, once achieved, could speak from any like-minded mouth. It was therefore a signal of spiritual prowess that one, or one's council, had a Speaker" (166). These Words Before All Else are not simply a prayer as is often given before public meetings or events in our contemporary American times. Indeed, the Speaker does not simply appeal to all sentient beings/spirits (ask for God's and the angels' blessing as a non-Native person might say), but those sentient spirit beings (animals, plants, waters, and so on) are called to and welcomed to the meeting by the Speaker (who has the ability to do so and thus earns her or him respect as a Speaker) so that universal consensus might be achieved. These beings are participants. The Speaker is not in a trance, is not channeling ghosts as the New Agers might say, nor is she or he not completely aware and present. The Speaker calls upon all sentient beings so that they too are part of the decision-making process, and communal ethics are upheld and respected. The notion of community to indigenous peoples is far more than merely human beings.

Another essential point to understand is gendering protocols that existed for most Native nations. Mann outlines the Iroquoian version thusly: "The gendering rule resulted in mirror-image councils of Clan Mothers balancing councils of male sachems. According to gendered protocol, men did not speak in women's councils and women did not speak in men's councils. Under this system of gendering, women sent male speakers to men's councils, while men sent female speakers to women's councils" (165). Because of this system of gendering to transmit information, great limitations existed for a EuroAmerican male ethnographer to gain knowledge about Native women's experiences, roles in their nation, and the women's story of her people. For example, traditionally it is simply inappropriate for a man to speak about the leadership, governing, sacred rites, clans, and so on of the women. However, when a male ethnographer came to a Native nation to get someone's story for a book about them and their people, only Native men would perceive it as socially acceptable to speak to the ethnographer because he was also a man. Hence Native women's stories are limited in this literary genre.

Furthermore, the accounts the Native male subjects told to ethnographers were the stories, experiences, traditions, and wisdom of the men, not the women. Unfortunately, ethnographers and a general readership did/do not realize the gendering protocol and simply assumed they were getting the "whole story" of the subject's culture when indeed they were only receiving, literally, half of it. In western culture, there are no gendering protocols, so the American ethnographers of the past simply assumed the Natives did not have them either. Here again the presumption of an ethnographer/writer that one Native person is representative of her entire nation and no other voices need to be heard to gain cultural authenticity is flawed thinking. Without the sufficient cultural knowledge, the ethnographer/writer simply cannot gain the story she or he is seeking because that requires experiential and complex traditional knowledge of the nation she or he is interviewing. In other words, cultural knowledge allows the interviewer and writer to ask the questions of the subject or of her or his writing that reflect cultural knowledge. An example of a culturally appropriate question to ask of a Native male subject would be, "Do the women have their version of this creation story or practice?" Conceptualization of a female universe complementing a male universe can be difficult for westerners to grasp. It is, at the very least, a brand new way of thinking for EuroAmericans about human systems, the cosmos, and human perceptions based in culture.

In most Native American autobiographies readers will find information that is seemingly about the whole nation when it is in fact only about the women or the men. For example, when Mourning Dove discusses beliefs about and practices in the lodge ceremony, she makes no mention that these are specific references to the women's lodge. The book's editor, Jay Miller, is familiar with Colville culture, so he knows to include discussion about gendering in the endnotes section of the book. The men's practices are not noted in her writing because, obviously, she is not a man and those practices are not for her to have knowledge about or discuss. We see this same event occurring in Black Elk's as-told-to story, as one does in nearly all the men's auto/ biographies written before and early in the 1900s. The Native men do not mention any of the women's ceremonies, practices, duties, or stories featuring them and their specific wisdom because they not only know little about them, but also, because of gendering protocol, it is not culturally appropriate for the men to discuss women's business. This point alone demonstrates a significant limitation in the Native American autobiographies in gaining a whole, complex, cultural picture of Native nations. Troubling enough is the realization that most Native autobiographies have been in circulation and widely read for decades, and readers, believing they are getting the "whole truth," have no awareness that a significant portion of the culture is utterly missing from the book.

Eurocentric understanding of Native languages and word choice is also highly problematic. For example, the English words "I" and "We" have far different meanings to a Native person than they do to a EuroAmerican. These different perceptions of meanings pose another challenge to communication between EuroAmericans unschooled in Native linguistics who interviewed Native Americans for their biographies. In the book *Native American Speakers of the Eastern Woodlands*, Mann discusses Native use of singular collective pronoun format and possessive pronouns. "I" means the individual speaker and her entire nation; "you" singular is the entire group she is addressing and "she" and "he" for all third parties (49). Mann offers this example but the bracketed information is my commentary: "I [the speaker's entire nation] return the hatchet he [the nation or audience being addressed] gave me" (49). Analysis of this linguistic practice among the Eastern Woodlands peoples in particular, and most other Native nations as well, demonstrates a life philosophy that is communal and seeks not to create division among people and other beings.

The notion of time is another significant difference between western cultural and Native perspective. Westerners see time and historic events as fixed and linear. Native perceptions of time are based on the belief that stories are living entities. Walter Capps calls this the "perennial reality of the now" that are "processes which are of eternal happening and recur in other cycles; there is no past, no present, no future" (*Seeing with a Native*...28). Native American scholar Gerald Vizenor describes the printed word as having "no evolution (like ancient to modern) in tribal literature; the word is there in trees, water, and air where it has been at all times" (*Narrative Chance*...x). One can easily imagine the difficulty this cultural difference alone creates between a EuroAmerican recorder/writer and a Native American story-teller. To a westerner, the concept of events perennially recurring, not being fixed, and existing within all other beings (trees, plants, air, and so on) is indeed a challenge to the very principles of that culture.

To the non-Native American, separating people into groups because they are ideologically in conflict (like political parties and religions), separating life events by the passage of time, separating ancestors from their descendents, separating types of beings from each other by grouping them into categories (like tree beings, animal beings, human beings, and so on) are all acceptable cultural notions. In academia, we separate epistemologies and methodologies into categories called departments where specific types of study are conducted. To Native nations, there is no separation of human ways of knowing and experiencing, albeit most nations have their unique way of understanding and expressing this interconnection. There is no compartmentalization, only interconnection and interrelationship so that the events of the "past" are as relevant and alive to those living beings today as they were when the events first occurred. For example, the proper care of Earth and Her waterways today ensures that future generations will inherit those actions and have clean water. This is NOT to be read as cause-and-effect theory, but as interrelationship and sentient memory. It recognizes that there is memory in the matter the universe is made of, and we are made of that matter and beholden to it, reaping what it contains or does not contain.

The issue of differing cultural perceptions of time is important to note because in EuroAmerican culture, Native traditions and peoples are often understood to be irrevocably eradicated, yet traditional Native people understand that belief to be false. As long as there is memory, and every living creature and element has memory, the traditions of Native peoples cannot be destroyed but may be re-called into this time period and expressed authentically once again.

Do the books *Black Elk Speaks* by John Neihardt and some of the other more popular Native autobiographical books like it (for example Frank Linderman's book *Pretty Shield: Medicine Woman of the Crow*) need to be absolute verbatim accounts of what the Native American interviewee spoke in order for the book or work to be of value? What value do these books have, if they have any worth at all, in sharing what the personal life and tribal experiences of the individuals interviewed were, and to whom do they have value? I would assert that these nations, as do all Native nations, have a far more traditional, relational, ceremonial, and thus important way of remembering their nation's history and people without the necessity of reviewing the EuroAmericans Linderman's and Neihardt's interview of one of their elders. Perhaps the greatest value of these autobiographical works created primarily by anthropologists in the 1800s is for the non-Native population to gain some knowledge of the indigenous culture. What information and cultural messages a EuroAmerican outsider garners from them is the problem.

The autobiographies published from the 1800s and early 1900s should be revised and rewritten to reflect Native cultural philosophy. Abundant information should be added in prefaces, appendixes, and words from nation-specific tribal councils about the Native subject of the book. The gulf in cultural beliefs between Native people and non-Native people is far too wide to allow Native American autobiographical works to speak for the Native individual her- or himself, or the person's national culture in general. The books defined within the genre Krupat named Native American autobiography should be used only in conjunction with more reliable sources (the stories and communal history rendered by Native American peoples and nations). Readers of this unrevised genre should bear in mind that they are witnessing the blending of antithetical cultures, and that the colonial, European culture is the one that had the final word on publication. Fortunately, that culture does not have the final word of the day. More and more, scholars are recognizing the limits of the genre and are entering into the discourse about it.

Autobiographies Featuring Native American Women

The last significant area of challenge for non-indigenous people in writing and reading about Natives in the Native American autobiographic literary genre is the disparity between Native and EuroAmerican cultures in their perceptions of women. The academic conversation about EuroAmerican and Native American cultural differences as demonstrated in early Native American autobiographies is incomplete without the deeper analysis of differences in perceptions of women between the cultures. Autobiographies featuring Native women are far less in number compared to autobiographies featuring men in this genre. Not only are they featured less as primary subjects, but less as prominent and complementary figures in the lives of the men who were interviewed for the books. Why is this so? I have already discussed the challenges of same-gendered communication, and there was certainly a dearth of EuroAmerican women ethnographers available to speak with Native women before the 1900s: that much is true. However, there is a deeper reason that Native women have been primarily overlooked in this genre, and in most scholarship, about Native peoples.

Remember that "scholarship" is still primarily created and perpetuated by EuroAmerican men and in the western historic past, since academia's creation, they were the sole creators, contributors, controllers, and definers of it. This is part and parcel of a patriarchal (male) structured social system. Thus, women were denied, until only recently, graduate-level education and opportunities for publishing their research. Biases against women still exist in the academy and pose serious obstacles for women scholars. Why then are scholars and the academy resistant to seeing who Native women were pre-European contact and who they still are today? The inability for the EuroAmerican culture to grasp who Native people are as a collective people lies in their inability, and great fear, to accept the roles, purposes, and being of Native women. This is because of the long-standing cultural biases against all women to which many men and women of EuroAmerican culture still cling. Native women's roles in their nations challenge those biases; thus, the importance of western scholars ignoring them is paramount.

In her definitive book *The Sacred Hoop*, Paula Gunn Allen defines a woman-centered social system (a gynocracy) as "...even distribution of goods; absence of punitiveness; relationship with nonhuman beings; powerful women are center of social well-being; and earth is considered an honored being" (Introduction). These characteristics are obviously missing from the prevailing culture of the United States. Hence, acknowledging their presence in pre-colonial cultures is a threat to the contemporary (patriarchal) cultural status quo that oppresses the very group that was once in power, namely women. Some examples of recent scholarship on matriarchies include: Makilam's *The Magical Life of Berber Women in Kabylia*; Shanshan Du's *"Chopsticks Only Work in Pairs:" Gender Unity and Gender Equality Among the Lahu of Southwest China*, and Peggy Reeves Sanday's *Women at the Center: Life in a Modern Matriarchy*. There are contemporary scholars who still go to great lengths to disprove the centrality of women in indigenous governing systems despite clear and unquestionable evidence in primary academic sources and the testimony and records of Native American nations.

It is evident that the refusal of the academy and scholars (both non-Native and Native American) to engage in serious discussion about the true cultural differences between Native Americans and EuroAmericans is that it challenges a deep-seated western cultural and religious belief about women. It would be difficult for any group that oppresses and silences another group to acknowledge that their victims are leaders within other cultural systems. This realization would not only be difficult to comprehend, but who would want to jeopardize their advantages and position of social power by admitting it is true and possibly affect the current regime? Also, it would be painful on the ego to admit that men's position of power was won by being culturally privileged based on gender, and not won from their sheer hard work and merit. So on the one hand, ethnographers of the past could hardly conceive of a woman-centered governing system or of a complementary gendered system, but, on the other hand, they would certainly not wish to publicize their discovery when at the time of publication of most as-told-to stories EuroAmerican women could not vote, go to college, own property, or control their own life trajectory. These are privileges Native American women not only enjoyed but solely controlled in many Native nations for millennia because complementary and gynocratic systems were/are understood to be the organic way of human life. Barbara Mann writes about this "clash of cultures" in regards to women in *Iroquoian Women* saying that, "[it] continues clouding the view to this day, for it is built into nearly every extant primary source, where it continues poisoning interpretations into the present..." (23–24). Even many Native American scholars cannot challenge the pervasive gender-specific (misogynist) cultural values to which they have assimilated.

As long as the history and traditions of Native women continue to be invisible to the larger American culture, the history and culture of all Native people will remain invisible. In other words, half the story will always be precisely that: part an historic account, part the culture, part the truth of the Native American people. To a colonial power, hiding its history of genocide and erasing the culture of the groups it oppressed is of course imperative.

A review of some contemporary defining theories about women's autobiographical writings in general is called for to illuminate this discussion. Editors Bella Brodzki and Celeste Schenck offer a variety of different approaches for the study of autobiography in their work *Life/ Lines: Theorizing Women's Autobiography* (1988). They note that "autobiographies...became central in wide-ranging critical and theoretical debate on the status of self, the nature of self-representation, of language. The serenely 'male' approach to those questions has by now been disrupted..." (x). Their work addresses the inclusion of all American women's voices into the overall EuroAmerican culture via their writing. Their focus is primarily on the notion of life writing, still quite different from the communal-focused Native tradition. The intention of life writing is to give voice to those who are silenced; but the purpose of Native narratives is to illumine the subject's national culture by demonstrating characteristics of it like communal ethos and gender complementarity. One hardly experiences the writing of American women to be representative of the patriarchal structure from whence it comes, but rather it is discourse to transgress against and challenge it. American women's writing was in the past published in spite and in defiance of their culture; even at times women writers assumed a man's name to ensure their work would be published. These are utterly foreign notions to traditional Native peoples and their nations who did not create, in pre-colonial times, oppressive systems that their people had to speak out against. Therefore, at their very foundations, life writing and Indigenous Communal Narratives are profoundly different in their intention, purposes, and final product all due to culture. Universalizing women's writing is cultural erasure; even contemporary Native women's personal narratives are ultimately for their people, not their sole personal benefit.

Germaine Bree writes in the book's foreword that "*Life/Lines* are rich in the wide diversity of routes by which women...have asserted their place as active subjects challenging the oppressive representation and actions of powerful hierarchies" (xi). Indeed, the book does what Bree notes, but Iroquoian women specifically, and most First Nations women generally, do not have to "challenge oppressive representations" and "actions of powerful hierarchies" in their nation of origin. Native women have always been "active subjects" in their nations and are understood to be the originators /Creators (Cosmic First Movers) of their worlds and consequently held, and still hold to some degree, positions of leadership. Second, most Native nations were not structured by hierarchies that had power concentrated solely in one gender—namely men, as in the western, patriarchal model. To the contrary, if any one gender had more power (as westerners would understand it) in indigenous governing and social structures, it was the women. Postcolonial experiences and systems created oppressive images of Native women, but this is traditionally not their experience. Therefore, life writing in order to move from social and personal silence to expressing one's life and the history of women is not appropriate or relevant for understanding Native perceptions of women.

In this same book, contributor Helen Carr's selection "In Other Words: Native American Women's Autobiography" raises issues about ethnographers' racism in collecting stories from Native women. She defines the central problem in reading any Native woman's autobiographical text as "interpreting a text in which a marginalized subject speaks a dominant discourse" (136). In First Nations cultures, especially the Iroquois, women were not marginalized. Marginalization only happened when a EuroAmerican, male ethnographer collected, or ignored, Native women's stories. Further, life writing still centers the self or the individual, which is not consistent with Native cultural beliefs or methodology. *Life/Lines* is an important literary work on EuroAmerican women's life writing; however, it is not relevant to the discussion of Indigenous Communal Narrative nor to Native women's oral transmissions and writings past, present, and future. The constructions, theories, and methodology presented in the anthology are appropriate and insightful only when applied to the writing of women in a non-Native culture. Hence, this work can neither be used to theorize on Native women's writing, nor to define it.

Literary Scholars of Native American Autobiography: Krupat, Sands, and Wong

There is much discussion and literary analysis published about the newly defined literary genre called Native American Autobiography. Unfortunately, most of the discussions and published works are Eurocentric and have significantly muddied an already culturally murky subject. The best known, popular, and published of the group of analysts in this field is Arnold Krupat. His were the first books published that eventually defined the genre. Works coming after his have all looked to his original guidelines, but have not gone much farther beyond his original parameters. Wong is the exception.

Following is a discussion about the work of each of the key literary analysts in this genre, and my comments in brief on their primary observations.

Arnold Krupat

In his book *For Those Who Come After*, literary scholar Arnold Krupat defines Native American Autobiography as "original bicultural composite compositions," which he distinguishes from autobiographies by Christianized Native Americans who could read and write English (30). Krupat is an influential literary scholar who has written extensively about Native American writing and writers. His work has made major contributions to the study of Native American literature, and he is the scholar who first defined the literary genre Native American autobiography. He more recently published additional works on the same topic entitled *Here First: Autobiographical Essays by Native American Writers* (2000) co-edited with Brian Swann, *Native American Autobiography: An Anthology* (1994) and *I Tell You Now: Autobiographical Essays by Native American Writers* (1987) co-edited with Brian Swann. In all these texts he primarily recounts much of the rubric and ideologies of his first text about Native American autobiography (*For Those Who Come After*) then adds a collection of autobiographical excerpts by Native North Americans.

Literary critic Lisa J. Udel notes that "the [1994] publication of Krupat's anthology is the first step in canon formation and consequently must be greeted with caution" ("Native American..." 177). She criticizes Krupat for the absence of what she names "Second Wave Resistance" writing by individuals in the American Indian Movement and many Native people who have written autobiographies, like former Cherokee Chief Wilma Mankiller, Russell Means, and Leonard Crow Dog (177). However, overall Udel praises his 1994 work and claims that it is "an interesting overview of the problems and pleasures of Native American autobiography" (177). The number of texts within this literary genre is somewhat limited compared to the numbers of autobiographical works there are by EuroAmericans in the same era.

Krupat notes that the emphasis of the Native American autobiographical genre is on the collaborative effort of speaker, translator, informant, writer, and many editors. In his first text on this genre, still considered definitive, *For Those Who Come After*, Krupat offers four categories of literary criticism of Native American texts and uses these concepts to analyze the genre he names Native American Autobiography. The categories are: Mode of Production, Author, Literature, and Canon. Krupat says that Native American texts are a result of "a complex but historically specifiable division of labor" (5) and that autobiographies of Natives were published by EuroAmericans in the early 1800s after the economy moved from agrarian to "production" (7); that Native North Americans used oral traditions as performance of stories, history, and sacred myth not as rote memorization of a fixed script, but a living translation and criticism all at once (11); and that in order for a Native American text to be authentic, it must come from a taped audition of Native performance and from a translator with fair working knowledge of the Native language. I will now address each of his categories below.

Krupat's "original bicultural composite compositions" description of books written by ethnographers from interviews of Native Americans (primarily from the 1800s) is misleading. The works would be original in that there are no others like them in the history of European literature; that much is true. If his meaning in using the word "original" is that the story originates from the Native American teller, that would be a misreading of Native culture which I discuss at length below. The terms "bicultural" and "composite" are also troubling because they imply equal time, contribution, and opportunity for the cultural expression of each contributor. The terms also suggest similar cultural expression and that the cultural beliefs and perceptions of both the EuroAmerican interviewer and writer and the Native American interviewee would be evident in the final text. A more accurate image is of a Native subject pressed into a EuroAmerican ideologic framework. Oftentimes explicit denigration of the subject and her or his nation is included in the most patronizing of terms by the ethnographer. Krupat's categories are insightful and have been important contributions to initially defining this genre, but they fall short of defining the very real cultural erasure created by the ethnocentric retelling of Native American people's lives in this literary genre.

Therefore, the "bicultural" portion of Krupat's definition does not entirely reveal all that is at work in this genre. So much of what is presented as authentically Native American falls considerably short of being a culturally accurate work. A better description of the Native American autobiographies of the 1800s would be Eurocentric, romanticized caricatures of Native Americans infused with some accurate retellings of Native history and personal Native narrative all presented in a western cultural context. Paula Gunn Allen offers an excellent study of how this happens in the article "Kochinnenako in

Academe: Three Approaches to Interpreting a Keres Indian Tale" in the spring 1985 issue of *North Dakota Quarterly*.

Krupat observes that this literary genre is another type of frontier where Native and EuroAmerican cultures meet. He claims that some ethnographers' practice (particularly Neihardt's) of changing even the tone of visions or historical accounts of a Native person puts a European cultural twist onto the story. This is the very type of twist that creates cultural stereotypes and misinformation, and, worse, cultural genocide, unfortunately. When the cultural voice of the originator is significantly altered, then the subsequent text is deeply flawed and not really "bicultural" at all, but a western, genocidal product producing stereotypes. A good source elaborating on "documentary genocide" is by Russell Booker in J. David Smith's work *The Eugenic Assault on America* (89–100).

Here now I will respond to Krupat's categories that have thus far entirely defined this genre:

Mode of Production. According to Krupat, two flaws delegitimize some Native autobiographical texts: the process of its creation and whether the writers received money for their creation. I argue that the process by which a so-called Native American autobiographical work is created does not determine accuracy or authenticity of the product. The manner in which the text was produced is not a measurement of the ethnographer's Native cultural education or expertise in methodology when interviewing someone of another culture. The process merely adds to the list of problems with this period-specific genre. Krupat discusses Native American texts as being a result of "a complex but historically specifiable division of labor" (5) and this either qualifies or disqualifies them with regard to accuracy and authenticity. Certainly the ethnographer/interviewer/writer of any Native autobiography from the 1800s benefited—significantly—from publishing his work, as Indian stories were very popular in both the academic community and general EuroAmerican society (37). Further, Native informants were often paid for their cultural information (7). Does that disqualify every product in this genre? Krupat argues that there are some texts which are legitimate, meaning not marred by monetary gain on either the interviewer's or interviewee's part. I argue that although production and payment are interesting issues surrounding this literary genre, they are insignificant compared to the far greater challenge of accurate cultural transmission.

If the mode of production included payment for the informant, and this determines the literariness of a Native autobiographical text, then most all information we have from ethnographic sources in this genre would be rendered inauthentic under Krupat's definition. His comments about mode of production raise issues about how authenticity is defined and by which culture's definitions authenticity is understood. This point is discussed under the author heading below.

Author. Native North Americans did (and still do) use oral transmission to tell the history, biographies, creation stories, and experiences of their nations and people. However, contrary to what Krupat asserts, Native Americans have always made use of written text, albeit the Native American version is quite a different invention from the European one. Native North American written text, specific to the Iroquois people, is called wampum. Wampum belts are made of stringed beads and can be read by someone who understands their language. Barbara Mann discusses wampum belts and beads in *Iroquoian Women: The Gantowisas* and notes that they "had ceremonial, spiritual, and political meaning and were, in fact, an indigenous form of proto-writing whose symbols were set and recognized throughout the woodlands" (100). Mann adds that the belts were "used in government and were documents tracing the lineage histories of the clans, minutes of meetings, and records of decisions reached or alliances created" (100). The renowned ethnographer John Heckewelder noted that "a good speaker will be able to point out the exact place on a [wampum] belt which is to answer to each particular sentence, the same as we can point out a passage in a book" (qtd. in *Native Americans, Archaeologists...*360). He personally witnessed the reading of wampum through attendance at council meetings, and this information is corroborated by ethnographic chronicler Daniel G. Brinton in *The Myths of the New World: A Treatise on the Symbolism and Mythology of the Red Race of America.*

In addition to wampum writing, there was also character writing (pictograms) on wooden sticks (*Native Americans, Archaeologists*...384) and stone tablets made by the Ohio Mound Builders (8). Heckewelder observes that northeastern Native nations had "certain hieroglyphics, by which they describe facts in so plain a manner, that those who are conversant with those marks can understand them with the greatest ease, as easily, indeed, as we can understand a piece of writing," claimed in *History, Customs, and Manners of the Indian Nations Who Once Inhabited Pennsylvania and the Neighboring States* first published in 1820. There were also pictograms and hieroglyphics carved into stone and trees throughout the eastern woodlands that can be characterized as signage and markers noting proper directions, the history at the place, and other information much like EuroAmerican signs along roadsides do today (360).

Charles C. Mann writes in *1491: New Revelations of the Americas Before Columbus* that "...MesoAmerican societies...created more than a dozen systems of writing" and that evidence of an indigenous writing system exists from 750 B.C. (216). He further notes that "what took the Sumerians six thousand years [to create a writing system] apparently occurred in Mesoamerica in fewer than a thousand" (216). Note that regardless of the medium in which the indigenous cultures wrote, be it stone, beads, or wood, the writing that was created and practiced came from a system of knowledge that was passed from generation to generation, and nation to nation, through their educational system. Ink on paper, the writing tools of humans from western culture, are no more sophisticated or legitimate than indigenous writing tools that consisted of strings of shaped beads, stone tablets, bark books, and pictograms on wood.

Thus Krupat's and most other scholars' of Native American studies claim that Native North Americans had no written text is incorrect. Unfortunately, unless any invention closely resembles the Europeans' version, the Europeans continue to believe that theirs is the only one created. Hence, Krupat claims that symbols-in-ink-on-paper is the only way to define "writing" and therefore literacy. What is implied in these presumptions is that Native North Americans were not civilized, evolved, or intelligent enough to write and read even their own language, which contributes to the EuroAmerican belief that Native people were (are) inferior to them. Further, it implies that western writing is superior to oral keepings. I do not believe that Krupat deliberately wishes to convey these blatantly racist meanings; nevertheless, this is the impression his point about a lack of writing system creates. A belief in a group's cultural and racial inferiority always plays a role in its colonizer's actions, i.e., the belief is necessary to make the colonization and genocide acceptable to the imperialist power. So it is no small point that Krupat is unaware of, and therefore does not mention, any and all Native texts which are part of that nation's culture along with oral transmission.

The conflict in literal translation versus interpretative meaning Krupat suggests in understanding Native North American authorship is problematic. He notes that the conflict in authorship of Native literature is translating either what was said or how it was said, which is an argument about literal translation versus the meaning of the story to the translator. Since Native American autobiographies from the 1800s were written by EuroAmericans, this is a profound assertion on Krupat's part. For a EuroAmerican translator of the 1800s (or today) even to suggest the meaning of a Native American's story without the necessary experiential, long-term, complex knowledge of a specific Native nation and its culture is ludicrous! The first necessary step the EuroAmerican translator must take is relinquishing the belief that her or his culture is the center (and best) of all human history and experience. For a EuroAmerican that is a mighty large step because the belief itself is a foundation of western culture. Therefore, the translator's work will most likely be a superficial product that, even with the best of intentions, almost unavoidably becomes a work transmitting ethnocentric biases in the place of real cultural knowledge. Therefore, neither literal translation nor the assumptions of a translator outside Native culture are adequate characteristics of an authentic rendering of Native American oral literature, as Krupat suggests. A working knowledge of the storyteller's language, and a profound, nonbiased understanding of the storyteller's Native culture are both requirements of authentic translation and transcription of Native oral literature.

Understanding the origination of Native stories is a point where Krupat is directly on target, and he is supported by contemporary scholars of Native American literature like Louis Owens, Gerald Vizenor, and Paula Gunn Allen. To communal people like Native North Americans, stories do not belong to or originate from the teller. However, just as quickly as he asserts this truth, Krupat contradicts himself by saying that subjects of Native autobiographies were their originators. Indeed, the Native subjects who told their stories to EuroAmerican ethnographers offered self-description in the context of their nation's history and experiences, but this is quite different from the heroic bragging committed in books by Daniel Boone, Davey Crocket, and Kit Carson. To suggest that Daniel Boone's autobiographical works are in the least similar to Lakota elder Black Elk's autobiographical stories is far off the mark. Boone and Crocket speak of their life events which render them unique and special heroes. Black Elk speaks of his visions for his Lakota people, for the well-being of his nation. The former is about the self as originator and the latter is communal; this is precisely what sets the two autobiographical forms (Native American and EuroAmerican) apart.

Krupat uses the term "augmentor" to describe ethnographers who changed the story they were told by a Native storyteller for the sake of clarity. This would describe what John Neihardt did with Black Elk's story. I would describe an augmentor's actions as deceitful both to the Native interviewee and to the readers of the book produced from the interview. Neihardt changed much of Black Elk's story: This is undisputed. The effects of those changes are significant if one wishes to know of Black Elk and the Lakota. Therefore, I would describe Krupat's term augmentor as something more like bad reporting that is culturally biased and misleads the book's readership.

Last, Krupat argues that authentic Native American texts from Native people of the pre-English speaking 1800s can only come from taped auditions and performances. First of all, he assumes again that what the EuroAmerican hears from these sources she or he will be able to understand and translate in a nonbiased, Native centered way. That is not the case, unless there is adequate academic and experiential knowledge of Native peoples and, ideally, a culturally identified

Native scholar is the one listening and interpreting. Second, it discounts the life of oral transmission and the living Native community of today! There is a sense in his statement that the real stuff is gone; that authentic Native narrative, experience, history, and culture are dead. This is the quintessential "Vanishing Red Man" stereotype. The subversive points in Krupat's observation is that Native people are gone; that those who still live cannot know the truth of the past; and that truth can be captured on a tape recorder. All three of these points are antithetical to Native beliefs. Further, this point of view is used against contemporary Native people and nations to delegitimize their traditions, identity, rights to sovereignty, and claims to land and mineral rights. Just as Native people have continued on after colonization, their traditions live on as well, albeit some are in different forms and expressions from 500 years ago. Nevertheless, they are still considered traditional and valid.

Literature. First, Krupat's reference to Wordsworth's belief that "the speech of the common person was literature" to support his own argument that oral literature is legitimate, implies that Krupat believes Native storytelling was not high-minded, poetic, and more formal than everyday language, but somehow common or ordinary language. Krupat's argument does not reflect the reality of the complexity, structure, and rich tradition of oral stories called Keepings. He seems to assume that Native storytelling, namely oral literature, would naturally be the same as everyday language; that Native oral transmission has no particular cadence, structure, word and phrase signifiers, or specially trained Keepers to distinguish it from everyday speaking. That is simply not so.

In his 1994 anthology *Coming to Light*, Brian Swann chronicles the vast and impressive practice of Native oral art and demonstrates its complexity, widely varying traditions, and history among indigenous peoples of primarily North America. To lift one example from this voluminous text for my purposes, I would like to note Jane McGary's points about oral tradition in her introduction to the oral stories "Raven" and "Fog Woman." McGary discusses features of oral literature by master storytellers, namely "pause structure and phrase length"

(93), and in doing so subtly presents an important point. There ARE many specific structures and characteristics distinct to oral storytelling rendering it quite unlike everyday language. Swann's anthology overflows with abundant examples.

In *Iroquoian Women: The Gantowisas*, Barbara Mann notes that Iroquois oral tradition is organized into four major traditions called "Keepings," and each is distinguished by subject, style, and word choice (30–31). The four traditions are: Truly Tales, Walking Tales, Spirit Stories, and Traditional Stories (30–31). Here is a brief description of each: (1) Truly Tales are factual and historical; the Keeper might begin with "Now, this truly happened." Often the story is told with a wampum belt, and the topic is of mundane, noncosmic matters. Minutes of council meetings, clan lineage, and national history are some topics written in wampum by the women. (2) Walking Tales are fictional. They might begin with "See the woman walking" or "It is as if the man was walking." They are also of a noncosmic topic. (3) Spirit Stories often begin "That woman went to the fields" or "That man went to the hunt." They most often end with spirit happenings and other ghost stories. (4) Traditional Keepings combine spiritual happenings and historical actions. These are the Epochal tales and traditions (30–31). They are the learning stories that transmit culture and are kept by Keepers who are specifically trained to tell these stories. Traditional Keepings are not told "around the campfire" by 'anyone' who wants to tell a story, but are told in a specific, ritual fashion. Mann notes, "Tales in all of these genres contain what folklorists and anthropologists call 'learning stories,' sophisticated analogies that make deliberate and conscious points about social principles, religious beliefs, and cultural values" (31).

To casually dismiss oral keepings as illegitimate, unreliable sources that are easily bested by a tape recording is akin to dismantling eons of Native cultures and replacing them with a thirty-second sound bite radio commercial and arguing for the validity of the recorded clip! What is recorded on audiotape cannot comprehensibly represent or illustrate the culture that is conveyed orally in the present day by a traditional Keeper. What the Keeper says is "more real" than what is contained on the tape recording, and more authentic, traditional and valuable to boot. Krupat believes that a tape recording of a dialogue from the past makes that dialogue, and thus the culture from whence it comes, legitimate. What he is missing, of course, is the realization that only EuroAmericans will think this is so, not Native Americans.

It is necessary to note these complex characteristics and traditions of oral stories first of all, because the necessity of demonstrating to non-Native peoples and to academia that oral tradition as a valid, definable genre unto itself is paramount. It is one of the very means by which indigenous peoples have been maintaining their culture for millennia. To consistently invalidate and perceive oral traditions as faulty sources of indigenous culture and history is not only to disrespect millions of human beings and their cumulative, albeit varying, cultures, but is also to continue the colonization process! Indeed, valuing oral keepings is no small point in the entire matter of valuing Native peoples. It is essential, key. Krupat's linking Wordsworth's comments about language of the common man to Native Keepings simply does not apply. The Native storytelling experience is distinct unto itself, and within the practice there are broad distinctions among Native nations.

Canon. The ancient songs, Keepings, and contemporary writing from members of Native North American cultures are, in small measure, taught at colleges and universities, but it is unlikely that they will ever be taught as worthy members of the American/western literary canon. Although they use the language (English) of the Europeans, and its mode of transmission (symbols in ink on paper), they are not representative of western culture, but rather of Native culture. Unfortunately, because of ethnocentric beliefs and most English departments' rigid adherence to their "English/White/Male/Western" canon, the written work of Native peoples is seen as a novelty at the university, an interesting tangent from a long-dead history of the overall American culture. Of course there are many individual faculty who challenge that position; however, considering the sheer absence of Native studies programs at liberal arts colleges, especially in the eastern

United States (there are none in the state of Pennsylvania!), it is easy to see that a problem exists.

Few universities regularly offer a course in Native American literature, but relegate its study to survey courses in American literature taught by professors who most likely have little to no scholarly expertise in the field. This means the Native American works are taught from a EuroAmerican point of view; that is to say, their primary themes and links to Native culture and history are missed entirely. A professor whose sole graduate education and scholarship area is in Native American literature would certainly not be permitted to teach a course in British literature or Shakespearean literature. However, the reverse is still considered acceptable.

The very definition of the western literary canon prevents Native written cultural expression from belonging. According to the *Bedford Introduction to Literature*, a literary canon is comprised of "those works generally considered by scholars, critics, and teachers to be the most important to read and study, which collectively constitute the 'masterpieces' of literature" (2100). The definition I note is that scholars, critics, and teachers determine what is included in the literary canon. Because the writing of Native Americans is so radically different from the writing coming from EuroAmerican culture, and most often offers sharp criticism and a history most EuroAmericans strive to ignore, its routine inclusion in college curricula is unlikely in the foreseeable future.

Neither Native American literatures nor the literature of women and people of color needs to belong to the canon to be taught at institutions of higher learning; that has already been proven, though the frequency of study of Native literatures compared to African American literatures still lags considerably behind in most college curriculums. Their combined offerings, including the literatures of all women, are still offered much less often than those courses whose literatures are written by men of Anglo-Saxon ancestry. However, rather than focus on Native literature's acceptance in academia (which may or may not come with time), Native writing and the college instructors of it should focus on studying Native people's work based on the standards set by Natives via their own cultural values and not define its worthiness by the model of the western canon. Native literary scholars, like Gerald Vizenor, have noted this for some time and argue that criteria for such a canon be determined by Native peoples. Indeed, the very characteristics which distinguish Native writing from the works of the western canon make it exceptional, so seeking homogeneity can only dilute the richness of the indigenous works and continue cultural erasure. An entirely separate canon of Native works, including live oral performance, is one way to celebrate and study the living cultures of Native peoples through their writing and stories. In another work by Krupat, *The Voice in the Margin* (1989), he offers in-depth discussion of issues around the Native literary canon and notes that the American literary canon in general should be flexible and define us as a people and culture (237). This is how we will enter the "cosmopolitan canon" (237). Unfortunately, as long as the department where literatures are read and studied at American colleges and universities is titled "English," the internalized belief is that Anglo-Saxon literatures, and their accompanying male-centered belief system, are the ideal and norm, and all other literatures are merely electives for marginal interest or entertainment.

Two foundational premises of Native American literature, as Krupat sees them, are "a global, ecosystemic perspective" and valuing oral transmission. I would add that a communal focus is the first and most important foundational premise of Native literature, along with the two he names. However, neither of the characteristics he names is present in the texts of the western literary tradition, so why would Native writers strive to belong in a western-cultural created institution that does not value who they are and what they value? Native American literature does not belong in the western literary canon because indigenous ways of knowing and expressing that knowledge are too radically different, and too complex, to fit into its limited frame. Writing within the larger cultural context of Native American and EuroAmerican is profoundly different based on culture, cosmology, social structures, ethics, and so on; and the many varying cultures and nations within those larger cultural contexts also have their own unique, written contributions. Expecting one to alter one's cultural expression to subscribe to the other's benefits no one. Further, it is a western cultural belief that differences threaten a community or system of belief and homogeneity is the ideal. In other words, Native cultures, especially in the Eastern Woodlands, perceived differences in opinion as safe to express within the community. Therefore, accepting different literary canons should only be enriching, not threatening, to English departments in America.

Scholar Martha J. Cutter wrote about Native literary canonical problems in a 1994 article about the autobiographical writing of Žitkala-Ša (also known as Gertrude Bonnin who was a Yankton Sioux woman and lived from 1876–1938). She notes that it is only when criticism of Native texts, the autobiographies in particular, are approached "in terms of how [they] subvert traditional modes of autobiographical and linguistic self-authentication that we can come to see its full richness and complexity, and understand the unique problem of a 'canonical' search for language and identity in Native American writing" ("Žitkala-Ša's..."). She adds that the autobiographies are often "judged deficient precisely because [they do] not conform to canonical models of autobiography." In other words, even when the quite popular works like Žitkala-Ša's writing are considered for admission into the western literary canon, e.g., when they are anthologized in a text of American Literature, the Native works are perceived as inferior because they do not have the constructions evident in works in the western literary canon. Cutter further argues that "Euro-American discourse and discursive structures have been used against Native Americans to promote their disenfranchisement, and so the white man's word, itself, is suspect." What she argues throughout the article is that Native literary canon formation continues to marginalize Native peoples, and Native women most especially, and that this is the primary challenge Native literary critics and academics face in this process of canonizing Native literature.

Kathleen Mullen Sands

In 1984, Kathleen Mullen Sands and Gretchen Bataille published a work addressing Native women's autobiographies titled *American In-*

dian Women Telling Their Lives. This scholarship addresses cross-cultural negotiations between a Native woman subject telling her story to a EuroAmerican ethnographer in primarily the pre-1900 era. Sands superbly discusses this complex relationship and offers an excellent history about the creation of these literary works. In a more recent article (1997) titled "Collaboration or Colonialism: Text and Process in Native American Women's Autobiographies" she notes that "collaborative autobiographies are not only intimate portraits of their narrators, but also, in sometimes subtle and sometimes blatant ways, portraits of their collector/editors" ("Collaboration..." 40). She then addresses the complex issues around this collaborative process in relation to gender.

Though Sands is a superb literary critic and scholar of things EuroAmerican, even in her more recent work she continues to impose those beliefs on Native peoples. She also points out that "life stories [were] ...collected before the advent of tape recorders...consequently almost no verbatim records of producer/narrators' encounters with collector/interpreters exist" (40). Though these are excellent observations and salient points based in the disciplines of anthropologic and ethnographic field work and literary criticism, they are ALL EuroAmerican perspectives! This maintains the English-department style point of view of the culturally superior western academic who continues to measure, categorize, and evaluate the testimony, life experience, and culture of people who are utterly unlike them in western cultural terms. Presenting Native testimony in this manner cannot be done and still possess any value to anyone in or out of the academy.

To begin, the stories of no Native person are "creative inscriptions of dialogues with the past"; they are such only to a person of western culture who perceives time and events as fixed, finished, over, and dead. Native people do not perceive events in this way. It is neither romantic fantasy nor culturally inaccurate to say that traditional Native cultures saw, and continue to hold, that all the people, events, and beings of the past are alive in some form and continue to influence and be part of our present, living community. The notion of "creative inscriptions" raises questions about cultural perceptions of truth and therefore validity of testimony. Sands seems to argue that only gainfully employed professors with research grants from our contemporary times have the self-appointed privilege of determining which indigenous testimonies of the past are true and which are not. The criteria they use, of course, would be based in Eurocentric belief and value systems. The Native cultural fact that most Native nations' Keepers change stories, even traditional sacred ones, as they determine is appropriate while keeping primary lessons and key events intact, does not seem to matter to contemporary literary critics who need everything on a tape recorder to prove its truth and therefore worth.

Second, conceptualizing events and memories of Native autobiographical subjects as "fictions," "real and imagined, accurate and inaccurate interpretations" is to impose EuroAmerican understanding of those notions onto a Native understanding of those notions. Her point suggests that there is only one way of understanding truth, time, memory, and how those notions are valued by a culture. EuroAmerican culture, again, perceives time and truth as things that are fixed, provable, and consented to by a public that can only acknowledge that there is one legitimate version of anything. In the article "Truth and the Hopi" by Andrew Wiget, he discusses that varying versions of traditions (sometimes even contradictory) are all equally true. Sands omits that what is considered valuable to a EuroAmerican culture, person, scholar, reader, or ethnographer is NOT what is important to a Native American. Literary scholar David Murray writes in *Forked Tongues: Speech, Writing, and Representation in North American Indian Texts* (1991) that "The concept of an individual life as an unfolding story which can be isolated, recalled and retold, made into a product for contemplation, is not one necessarily shared by other cultures, and in particular not by oral cultures" (65).

Last, just as Arnold Krupat suggests where we can find accuracy in the telling of Native stories and culture, Sands also argues that accuracy can be disclosed via a tape recorder. As I responded to Krupat on this point, I will say again that this position implies that the real thing is gone (Native culture and Native people): an entirely EuroAmerican cultural point of view. It also suggests that truth must and can be fixed (as on paper, audio, and videotape) and that what has been fixed in time by these means can then be qualified as "real" and "authentic." Of course, it is only qualified as real and authentic to EuroAmericans; Native peoples already know what is real and authentic to their cultures without the necessity of a tape recording privileging just one story from someone of their nation!

At every turn of Sands's analysis, she imposes EuroAmerican thinking onto the lives and means of communicating life experience of Native peoples. Her analyses are western culturally and academically excellent, and can certainly speak to those in that institution, though it only obscures not illumines Native cultures. However, although Sands has deconstructed the obstacles and cross-cultural issues in this literary genre so keenly, she has really only created another obstacle that obscures the analysis of it: western cultural academic jargon about Native peoples.

At the article's end, she urges "those who teach and write in this field...to be well prepared to analyze both the earliest and latest forms of Native women's autobiography in the light of feminist theory; post-colonial awareness; ethnographic self-reflexivity; speech act, genre, and inscription theories; interdisciplinary performance; and cultural semiotics" (54). Whew! In other words, the ethnographers of today should engage in as many EuroAmerican academic constructions as possible in order to continue the problems already present in this genre to further dilute and misrepresent indigenous peoples. She then urges literary scholars to "follow the lead of ethnographers and go into the field in order to experience firsthand the complexities of bi-cultural inscription" (54).

What she is prescribing is a glossier version of the same mangled genre we now have dubbed "Native American Autobiography." Her insistence that ethnographers simply need to clean up their act when they are out in the field completely misses the point: Native peoples do not need ethnographers to tell their stories! Indeed, some Native peoples often refer to the annual summertime presence of academics in their communities and on reservations as being descended upon by mosquitoes: They just never go away. Native peoples tell their own stories in writing now; and many do not feel the need to tell non-

Native peoples about their culture at all: a stunning point to a westerner. This is because indigenous peoples do not have the belief that their culture, stories, or people can be lost forever as EuroAmericans believe can happen. Herein is a profound difference between the cultures.

Hertha Sweet Wong

An important contributor to the discussion of Native American Autobiography is scholar Hertha Sweet Wong. She describes her work, *Sending My Heart Back Across the Years,* as "a detailed consideration of a select number of distinctly native traditions of self-narration and their later interaction with Euro-American forms of autobiography" (4). She notes that the so-called definitive works of scholars of Native American Autobiography, which include the well-known Gretchen Bataille, Kathleen Mullen Sands, and Arnold Krupat, "negate the possibility of pre-European contact tribal traditions of personal narrative" (4). Wong continues to point out that each of the scholars mentioned uses a Eurocentric approach to the study of Native American autobiographies and thus their work is off-base. Though this may not appear to be that great of a scholarly crime, when one considers the enormous social problems Native Americans still face today because of hundreds of years of stereotyping and colonization via American literature and academic scholarship, their scholarly biases appear quite troubling. As long as the adults (teachers, professors, and scholars) continue to teach the children (students) European ways of thinking about and studying Native peoples, non-indigenous Americans and the non-indigenous world will never relinquish its racist perceptions and biases of Native cultures of the past or Native communities of today. Therefore, the seriousness of continuing to characterize Native cultures in EuroAmerican terms in academia is significant. These stereotypes are being passed from one generation to the next as surely as racist beliefs about African Americans were taught in the academy in the past.

Wong's excellent book examines in detail the non-written form of indigenous pictographs (drawings on cave walls, buffalo robes, and indigenous art in general) and demonstrates how these pictographs are self-narration and therefore pre-Columbian autobiographies. She names the purpose of her work to "expand the Eurocentric definitions of autobiography to include non-written forms of personal narrative and non-Western concepts of self and to highlight the interaction of traditional tribal modes of self-narration with Western forms of auto-biography" (5). Unfortunately, she too makes the common error of saying that indigenous peoples had no written language. Considering that Wong's work solely addresses nations west of the Mississippi (Plains Indians, Cheyenne, Crow, Winnebago, and Lakota), it is not surprising that she is perhaps unaware of the history and culture of the nations of the Eastern Woodlands, and of many others that had systems of writing. The peoples east of the Mississippi had complex systems of writing, as I have already noted.

From the pictographs reproduced in Wong's book, it is clear that the work is also communal as the experience of the self of the artists certainly reflects the experiences of their nation as well. Herein lies the defining point that Wong addresses and Krupat seems to miss: whatever the indigenous individual expresses, it is only in the context of her or his community. The autobiographer cannot, and should not, extract the story of the individual from the nation. This is Eurocentric and is the beginning of a flawed Native autobiographical prod-uct/story. Wong describes this as "Instead of emphasis on an individual self who stands apart from the community, the focus is on a communal self who participates within the tribe" (14).

Unlike the work of major contemporary scholars like Krupat, Sands, and Bataille, Hertha Wong's book *Sending My Heart Back Across the Years* is an excellent example of Native-centered scholarship that reflects a complex understanding of western and Native cultural differences.

There has been much discussion, and many publications about Native American Autobiography have appeared since Krupat dubbed the ethnographic literary artifacts as such in the 1980s; however, the heart of the matter continues to be overlooked. How can these books now serve Native nations? How can they teach all American peoples, both college students and a general readership, about EuroAmerican colonial history in the United States and the complex cultures of the Native North Americans? The answer is right before us: revision of the biographies. The foundation work has been accomplished. Literary scholars and Native American academics have reviewed these books to note where their limits lie; that much is true. Now it is up to the present and next generation of writers to shape these works into authentic articles of nation-specific Native culture. This is the next step.

❧ CHAPTER TWO
Indigenous Communal Narrative

In this chapter the new possibilities and approaches for the study of autobiographical works about Native Americans who lived before and shortly after the year 1900 are presented. Following the guidelines below will enable writers and researchers to evaluate Native American autobiographies currently in circulation and create works of Indigenous Communal Narrative. These guidelines disclose what re-visioners of Native American autobiography should strive to create from these already published texts.

The categories created by Arnold Krupat for the study of autobiographies of Native Americans from contact to the early 1900s are only a start in addressing this complex genre. The rubric offered in this chapter is intended to be a new way of understanding and envisioning works that have been dubbed Native American autobiography, and should be used as a revised guide to evaluating interviews, biographies, and autobiographies of Native Americans collected and written by ethnographers, and for new works that are written in the future about the life of a deceased indigenous person. Around 1900 Native Americans began primarily doing their own writing and did not have to rely on English-speaking people to publish their history, stories, and autobiographies. Today the Native American autobiography genre from the 1700s, 1800s, and early 1900s is still used. EuroAmerican writer Richard Erdoes is a prominent, and albeit controversial, contemporary autobiographer and interviewer of Native North Americans. Some of his most famous works published are interviews of Archie Fire Lame Deer, Mary Brave Bird, and Leonard Crow Dog. In addition to this is the emerging genre Indigenous Communal Narrative. Native scholars Paula Gunn Allen, Maurice Kenny, and Jay Miller have made significant contributions to the Indigenous Communal Narrative genre with their comprehensive works about Pocahontas (2003), Tekonwatonti (1981), and Mourning Dove (1990), respectively.

Who benefits from these Indigenous Communal Narratives? If the Native American autobiographies are revised and sufficiently added to, and more closely resemble a work of Indigenous Communal Narrative, that is with a mind intent on honoring Native culture, then it is a benefit to both the Native American and non-Native nations, but certainly for different reasons. Native people need their history and culture to live with dignity and purpose: to stay alive and live meaningfully, to continue the circle of life that began with their ancestors. That information is given through oral performance and contact with one's Native community of course, but can certainly be enriched through book learning. A book that represents Native culture and accurately reflects Native history and origins will ultimately dispel the long-standing stereotypes prevalent in contemporary American society, still to profoundly detrimental effect. Evidence of the significant challenges facing indigenous nations is in every issue of the Native owned weekly newspaper *Indian Country Today* and all are results of colonization. To have books honoring and correctly reporting on Native culture and history become part of American mainstream culture and its educational system can only have a positive effect, just as books about African American experience have done.

Non-Native people also need the books to bring meaning to their lives on Turtle Island (North America). This is one reason why the earliest Native American autobiographies continue to be so popular among American readers; they offer a rich and beautiful philosophy and way of life that western culture and modern lifestyles simply cannot provide. Non-Native Americans need healing from the devastation they designed and enacted from first contact to the American Indian holocaust of the 1700s, and with the biological warfare that their ancestors waged during colonization that culminated in the American Revolutionary War. Colonization of indigenous peoples continues unto today in a variety of ways. The Eurosettlers are broken too from the crimes against Native people, and as long as those crimes remain hidden, no one can heal: neither the perpetrators nor the victims. What this means is that America will remain a broken land until the crimes of the past are acknowledged.

In *Seeing with a Native Eye*, Walter Capps says, "Americans in general are disenchanted, confused, misaligned, and overwhelmed… and need restoration with the universe," and this is why so many look to Native American religions for "restoration and a sense of identity" (4). He wrote this in the 1970s and, unfortunately, one might argue that this state of disenchantment has only become more of a widespread and deeply seated disease among Americans as they grow farther away from the values of the original inhabitants and their connection to each other and to Earth. Mary Daly claims that "the necrophillic leaders of our phallotechnic society destroy the earth" (*Gyn/Ecology*…21), and in her newest book *Amazon Grace* she offers detailed philosophic and hard-to-ignore evidence from scientists and social commentators about the denigration and soul loss in American society. Where she looks for an answer is to the philosophy of the Native Americans as espoused via the nineteenth century writer/suffragist Matilda Joslyn Gage, an adopted EuroAmerican member of the Mohawk people. Daly and her contemporaries argue that returning to a philosophy of communal values where the whole of life (humans, animals, plants, waterways, and so on) is held in high regard is the only way for our world to continue. Native culture is obviously a culture of life and beauty. Is it any wonder then why study of this literary genre remains pertinent, timely, and relevant to today's and to future generations?

What should be the foremost objective in rewriting or analyzing any previously written Native American autobiography, or a new work of Indigenous Communal Narrative about a deceased Native person, is that a reader can pick up the book and be significantly and accurately taught about Native culture. Books that perpetuate stereotypes of Native Americans must become easily recognized as outdated and false. They should not be discarded, but join the ranks of other American-authored books that espoused stereotypes, bred and justified hatred, and falsified the history of non-EuroAmericans, women, and other groups in North America. For example, one day most Americans should be able to look back on previously published stories about Pocahontas and instantly recognize them as flawed, just as most Americans can now easily recognize the flaws in the portrayals of African Americans in publications and former national policies about them. One day EuroAmericans may find caricatures and images of buck-toothed "Indian chiefs" on sports, automobile, and clothing logos as offensive and dated as similar former images of African Americans as "Aunt Jemimas" and "Sambos" are today. These caricatures of African Americans are primarily banished from most corners of EuroAmerican culture or are at least seen as sources of embarrassment in mainstream culture; however, it is still acceptable to portray Native Americans in such demeaning, stereotyped ways. Public recognition of the offensiveness of the African American images was brought about by general education campaigns attacking racist stereotypes and was the cause for such progress. Indigenous Communal Narratives can be important tools in an effort to do the same for Native American peoples.

In order for a sway in public perceptions to happen, there must be a significant pool of works that tell the truth about Native people, so that the general American public can begin to see Native people and history as they truly are. Reversing the damage done by centuries of misinformation via the Leather Stocking Tales, deep-seated historic lies, racism, and the dying culture theme of James Fenimore Cooper's *The Last of the Mohicans* (Pearce 199–203), is a good beginning and can be successfully accomplished through the unique culturally aware and culturally complex literary product that revised Native American autobiographies and Indigenous Communal Narratives offer.

A resource for doing so already exists thanks to H. David Brumble III who in 1981 wrote *An Annotated Bibliography of American Indian and Eskimo Autobiographies*. Though Brumble does not engage the reader in a discussion about indigenous communal ethos and appropriate collaborations for creating a work that can be called indigenous, and therefore an authentic source on Native culture, his work is a solid starting place for the scholar who wishes to create an authentic Indigenous Communal Narrative. Many of Brumble's annotations do not reflect, or even suggest, the importance of collaborative work between the text transmitted from the Native subject in the past with

Native elders, scholars, and tribal councils of today. Indeed, his point of view remains similar to that of his contemporaries who are primarily interested in verifying for the sake of literary authenticity the transmission of the text. There is much discussion in his annotations about whether the subject's testimony is considered accurate, real, or accepted by ethnographers and academics of the subject's era and of today. There is analysis about the intrusion of the ethnographer/writer into the testimonies of the Native subject, but there are no suggestions about how to undo the problem or remake the auto/biographies. The works are primarily evaluated solely on how they are presented as is. This has value only for the purposes of academic discussion and certainly has no real impact on contemporary Native peoples and the tremendously negative effects of colonization they still endure. In the end, the stereotypes created and perpetuated by these texts must be dispelled and revising the auto/biographies of the past have real and lasting potential for doing so.

In sum, the reason for the necessity of a discussion of works written by EuroAmericans based on the lives of Native Americans is that what has been produced in the past is superficial and inaccurate. If any colonized people are to regain their history externally (meaning an accurate rendering of that history in the dominant culture) and thus their status within the colonizer's new nation, they must be able to say who they are, where they came from, and what really happened during colonization: and they must be believed. In order for the non-colonized society to believe them, the colonized peoples must be taken seriously and respected. Native American Autobiography at its revised best and Indigenous Communal Narratives accomplish the task that Native American autobiographies have only failed to do: They make the Native person and her or his community real, disclose the richness of Native culture and its great complexity along with all the history and traditions of its people. They also, most importantly, make clear that the Native nation and its language, culture, and governing systems still exist. This is essential to demonstrate.

Here then are the primary considerations important both to produce and evaluate autobiographies and biographies already written by EuroAmericans in collaboration with Native Americans primarily before the 1900s, as well as works compiled for a Native American historic icon (like Tekonwatonti, Pocahontas, Chief Joseph) by a contemporary writer of Indigenous Communal Narrative. The first four criteria might be best addressed in the preface or introduction to such books so readers know precisely what they are about to read in ways that they really should know.

Primary Considerations for Evaluation of Texts

The cultural background and education of the interviewer and writer must be known. Is she or he Native American, and if so, from what nation? Is the writer culturally identified? How is that demonstrated? Is it the same nation as her or his subject? Does the writer have scholarship in Native American studies: either self-directed, through the subject's own nation via Native story keepers/ historians, or from an institution of higher learning? With whom did the writer study? Can she or he speak, write, and/or comprehend the subject's Native language?

The autobiographer must consult Native American elders, story keepers, writers, and scholars for their guidance. What does the subject's Native nation say about the work and what do other Native literary scholars have to say about it?

Was the interview conducted in the Native person's language or were there multiple translators? Who translated?

If the book was published long ago, who was the publisher and what was the editorial process? Was the Native subject involved in that process? How much was the subject's story changed and by whom? Discussion of this point by contemporary literary critics (some of whom should be Native American) might be included for further amplification.

For works compiled after the Native subject's death, the writer must be able to recognize and translate primary sources that could be and often are prejudicial and inaccurate. Adequate Native-centered and/or western cultural style scholarship and experience in the field would be essential on this point.

Knowing what Native elders, nations, scholars, and writers say about a previously published autobiographical work on a Native person is essential in evaluating it as authentic, characteristic of that nation's culture, and therefore legitimate.

Does the nonfiction work or poetry collection reflect the cultural philosophy of the subject's Native nation? For example, most Native nations are communal-centered; does the work allow for a number of voices to speak about the subject and for themselves and their history? This is essential if the work is defined as Indigenous Communal Narrative. Important to note is that communal does not mean individual Native peoples were without pride in their merits and talents and that they were not held in respect for them by their nation. Indeed, the variety of different medicine doctors; Keepers of the nation's stories that include historic, sacred, and everyday happenings and teachings; Speakers, Clan mothers, chiefs, war chiefs; and a number of other titles, duties, and offices within the nations were all earned by individuals who were uniquely qualified for such duties. These cultural practices defy the popular belief that the communal cultural philosophy of Native nations prevented any expression or practice of individuality and that theirs was/is merely a collective identity. That is quite untrue to the extent that the individual expressed her or himself above and outside of their nation. Instead, Native individuals expressed their uniqueness or special qualifications, talents, and abilities as integral, interconnected members of the entire biosphere they inhabited. For example, to name an exemplary plant medicine doctor as above or apart from her community because of her unique talents is to cut her away from her cultural system of being, which is a western cultural point of view. Within the safety and for the benefit of the community, uniqueness was expected. This differs from western cultural expressions of individual talents because the benefit of the community is not expected, and the purpose of the special talent is to solely exalt the individual so he stands apart from the community.

The work of Indigenous Communal Narrative must include accurate portrayals of Native and colonial contact, and be grounded in Native experience of that contact. A chronology of historic events pertinent to the Native person's nation, and simultaneous events outside the nation that affect them, should be included. This might best appear in an appendix showing dates in American history that include: key American and European political policies affecting the Native nation; laws passed that dictated Native removal from ancestral lands onto reservations; treaties signed and broken; life span and titles of key Native leaders during the subject's life; and the dates of primary non-Native officials, whose policies affected the Native nation, and who held office. What such a chronology would do is place the Native subject of the book within the events of the local and world communities around her or him, and thus offer readers an important perspective of happenings that affect and are relevant to the subject's life.

The writer of the book must possess an understanding of the relationship Native people have with the earth and all other non-human beings, and how it affected and played a significant role in the subject's life. The nation's creation story should be included in the text, along with Native analysis of it. Creation stories define human social structures that include far more than religious beliefs. Notions of gender, and social and personal power based in gender, are often revealed in the events of a nation's creation myth. Further, a people's way of conceptualizing life and all the systems of life can be found in their origins stories. Therefore, this story and all related origins stories should be included in an Indigenous Communal Narrative, so readers can witness how the subject's life unfolded within her or his nation's system of knowing. The story might be explicitly stated in an appendix, or amplification notes might be added to an already published autobiography explaining the subject's first mentioning of a tradition that is linked to the creation story. Clan structures, beliefs about human and other being relationships (like human and plant relationships, for example), ideas about relationship with the earth, and all governing structures stem from creation stories as well. Their inclusion in the Indigenous Communal Narrative is imperative if writers wish to transmit adequate cultural knowledge to their readers.

The writer must understand the complex social, economic, cosmologic, and political structures of the subject's nation and must reflect that understanding in the production of the book. A lengthy discussion disclosing the relationship among clans, clan membership, clan roles, and so on is imperative because Native clan systems are key to the functioning of their nations. How councils were and are determined and their functions in the nation, as well as the existence of speakers and their protocols, is also important. The ways leaders were chosen and their length of office is essential as well. What this information brings to the Indigenous Communal Narrative is a legitimization of Native nations and cultures. Simply presenting Native people as primitively existing without any means of government, formal education, and social structures portrays them as not being competent to create or sustain such systems. Indeed, the Native American autobiographies currently in circulation that were written by ethnographers precisely convey that image. Readers of these texts would naturally assume that Native peoples had no cultural systems at all, but just sat around on the prairie, warred with their neighbors, and hunted buffalo! Including information about the highly complex social systems of the subject's nation would shatter that stereotypical falsehood.

In addition to the points above, the writer must also strive for these gender-specific goals if authenticity is to be obtained. They are conditions for the work *whether for a female or male* Native American subject: The writer must be fully aware of the severe biases held in western culture against women and how these biases might color the writer's work. This approach requires truthful and brave self-examination and examination of EuroAmerican culture that may be quite difficult for a writer still in denial about western cultural misogyny.

The writer needs to have full possession of the social, political, economic, and cosmologic structures of the interviewee's nation in relation to gender. If EuroAmerican prejudices are transparent, then the writer will have a far easier time achieving this mandatory point.

The writer must strive to portray the Native woman as a Native woman, not a European woman in feathers and blankets. For example, if the Native woman has many children by several men, the culturally uneducated biographer might describe her as sexually promiscuous based on western cultural beliefs about women and sexuality. Most likely to the contrary, the subject's culture places no such constraints, judgments, or negative perceptions on women and their childbearing and sexuality. So this example would be an inaccurate portrayal of the Native woman subject's life based on the EuroAmerican belief in the male ownership of children and male control of women's sexuality.

Even the most honorable scholar with the best of intentions cannot revise an authentic product of Native American Autobiography or write an Indigenous Communal Narrative if she or he does not have the sufficient Native cultural education. The "honor" and "intentions" of an ethnographer have all too often been the downfall of the Native American subject, even when the individual had the noblest goals in mind (the so-called preservation of Native culture). To the Native people, culture, and keepings cannot and need not be saved by non-Native people. The pre-European contact ancient culture, sacred teachings, and history of the First Nations can be and are accessible, albeit by a far different medium from the one the EuroAmericans believe is real or legitimate. The teachings are carried in the collective memory and practices of the Native peoples living today.

Dreaming, spiritual travel, visions, and spirit guidance in ceremonies and rituals are all ways of knowing and learning valued by indigenous peoples. Information gained from reading wampum, baskets, pottery, bark books, artwork, animal hides, beadwork, and so on are all legitimate ways of remembering tradition and cultural knowledge. Therein knowledge is transmitted to its seeker or Keeper. This knowledge is alive, is still at work within Native communities today, and is known by their Keepers. As Barbara Mann says, "...is hovering at the edges of consciousness, waiting to re-emerge from the dark night of eclipse" (*Iroquoian Women* 358). Indigenous Communal Narratives are one way Native cultural information can begin their reemergence into mainstream world cultures. Why say "reemergence?" Because indigenous cultures were the primary and only cultures of Turtle Island before colonization. May they gain their voice at the national council table once again as they rightly deserve.

Defining Indigenous Communal Narrative

Paula Gunn Allen's definition of communal narrative in the preface of this book began the discussion of what I am now suggesting to be "officially" categorized as a new literary genre. The word "new" means: new to the academy, an institution that was created out of the mind of western culture and brought to North America by the Europeans. Indigenous people have always engaged in a variety of methods of telling the stories, history, and business of their people, albeit in very different forms from the Europeans. This is how a literary work that is defined as an Indigenous Communal Narrative might be created. The example of Miller's work at the end of this chapter and of Maurice Kenny's poetry collection about Tekonwatonti in chapter six illustrate these points precisely.

To begin, an academic scholar would describe an Indigenous Communal Narrative as interdisciplinary. This means it draws on the ways of knowing and reports on information across the academic disciplines, which may include history, economics, gender studies, politics, environmental studies, astronomy, psychology (personal relationships), literature, and social structures and perceptions. This is how an academic would define and create categories, but of course this is not the Native way of doing things or of thinking. In other words, the work would allow the voices of these cultural characteristics to speak in ways that represent indigenous ways of knowing. They would demonstrate interconnection and interrelational existence among the whole of life. Indeed, we would need to hear this information in order to understand the entire community around the subject of the book. The work could not simply report the individual's personal preferences and notable experiences of life, but must seek to present the community as it was when the subject lived, reporting on the beliefs and structures of the Native person's nation. The individual's life would reveal her or his culture, and this is precisely the goal of the work: a window to understanding a Native nation, not merely one Native person. This type of presentation would then require readers to critically think about the individual and gain an even deeper understanding about the subject's life, motives, beliefs, and actions. Including the reader as a participant in revealing the Native subject's experience, and subsequently her or his nation, is Native methodology that values the responsibility of all people to arrive at understanding and conclusions themselves without the final lessons/information merely being overtly spoken or handed to them.

The voices included in an Indigenous Communal Narrative would be those beings valued by the subject's culture. For example, perhaps a primary first experience and relationship to a person of an indigenous nation whose citizens highly value rattle making would be the subject's first rattle. The writer/ethnographer would need to know that and thus ensure that information is in the book. Perhaps Native children's primary male relationship is with their uncle, not the biological father (as it is with most Woodland nations). Information about that relationship might be important to include in the work because Uncle would be a significant relationship in the subject's life and contain large metaphoric implications. People in the subject's immediate family and within the larger nation are equally important, though for different reasons, and they should all appear in the book. Information about the subject's relationship with non-human beings would also be appropriate, and how those relationships are understood within the subject's national culture. For example, the relationship between someone who gathers plants for medicine and the plants themselves might be discussed. Are there traditional songs sung to the plant at the time of collection? Are they collected at a particular time of year? Inclusion of this information is not simply for interest, though it would of course be interesting to readers, but through this information readers can witness the complexities and profound wisdom in the traditions that characterize all Native culture. This recognition then creates in the reader respect and appreciation for Native peoples and also offers a new way of perceiving and being in relationship with Earth. Both outcomes are extremely important in our current times as Native nations and Mother Earth are both facing enormous challenges to their existence.

Relationship with Earth is also important, and what that means within the subject's national culture. Among most Native nations, particularly in the northeast, the notion of Mother Earth is part of their cosmology. However, not all Native nations refer to or understand Earth to be Mother Earth. Nevertheless, relationship with Earth is foundational to all Native peoples, so ensuring information about that relationship, particular to the subject's nation, is included. Mother Earth should not be conceptualized in endnotes or appendixes as an "it," but rather as a living, sentient, intelligent being before whom all life is humbled. When the auto/biographical subject discusses perceptions of Earth and cultural relationship with Her, such information should be presented to readers in reverential terms. This approach demonstrates cultural respect on the editor/writer's part and will therefore ask respect from the reader. What the Indigenous Communal Narrative does is model appropriate behavior towards Native people and nations, along with the history and cultural information it supplies.

Including in the Indigenous Communal Narrative voices of the subject's national leaders at the time of her or his life creates a comprehensive historical and cultural picture for readers. Denoting offices, election, and appointment processes of leaders will also garner deeper understanding of the subject's culture and command respect from readers. The events occurring during the subject's life that affected her or his nation are important to include. A chronology of events in an appendix, along with biographical information of Native leaders would be helpful. Putting these events in context with European settlement of Turtle Island would then add an even more comprehensive view highly beneficial to readers. It is also crucial in many Native cultures to know the past (and future) lives of the subject. Reincarnation, as specifically understood in Native cultures which is radically different from Eastern notions of Karma, is shape shifting. It occurs within lineages, clans, and nations as the community has need of the individual's talents (*Iroquoian Women*...333–35).

Inclusion of the Creation story of the subject's nation is imperative, along with an indigenous analysis of that story. Connections with the Creation story and the roles of the subject's life, sociopolitical structures, and national economics would be important as well. From human cosmologic stories perceptions about life, life relationships (human, plant, animal, stars, and so on), and social systems are constructed. Here is where a writer must begin chronicling the life of a Native person to ensure cultural authenticity. The creation story is where the primary beliefs of human individuals and societies are constructed and shaped. Beliefs about gender, power, and the ordering of the universe lie within the events of a people's creation story. Unfortunately, unless the creation story of an indigenous nation is explicitly stated and discussed in a communal narrative, non-Native readers will automatically assume that their belief systems apply to Native peoples. Of course, this is not true at all.

Any literary work defined as Indigenous Communal Narrative should leave the reader not only with information about one Native person, but should be a teaching about that person's nation: its history, its culture, its values and ethics, and sociopolitical structures. The writers of these works should strive for wholeness at all times and a final product that demonstrates Native methodology. What readers should gain is a sense of knowing the Native subject's cultural "wiring" so that her or his very culture is clearly revealed. A sense that the story is ongoing is also important; the story of a Native person neither begins nor ends with that individual. It began when her or his people were created and it ends when we all end (or when the elders say it ends). Indigenous Communal Narrative is the answer to the serious problem of continuing to sell the idea, via Native autobiographies like *Black Elk Speaks*, that all Native nations are homogenous, male-centered, doomed by colonialism, and unable to speak for themselves.

Review of Indigenous Communal Narrative Criteria

A work qualified as an Indigenous Communal Narrative features a single life testimony of an indigenous person that simultaneously reveals the culture of that individual's Native nation. The subject should appear to readers as clearly a part of her or his community, not separated or extracted from it. Notable leaders, historic events, and individuals involved in the subject's life should be represented from the Native perspective. The creation story of the subject's life should be presented with Native-focused interpretation and commentary. The work should reflect indigenous ways of knowing and express them in a legitimatizing manner. The voices of non-human entities should be presented in the work as well, for they too are part of the subject's community. Inclusion of a glossary of terms explaining words and phrases used in the subject's language is important, just as a chronology of relevant historic events and brief biographic information of leaders and persons important to the individual is important to ensure a culturally comprehensive finished product.

A Few Words About Methodology

Understanding present problems in research about Native Americans generally and Native literary works specifically is important to the study about Native American autobiography and Indigenous Communal Narrative. How research is conducted and interpreted, previous misconceptions based on culturally biased literature, and the implications this all has on Native communities, plays a role in interpreting works in the literary genre Arnold Krupat named. Though Krupat, Brumble, Sands, and other literary analysts have adopted the perspective of Native American autobiographies as literary artifact, this point of view cuts Native people out of the equation and thus perpetuates merely an academic discourse. Academic discourse may shine a bit of light into the racist, exclusionary corners of academia, particularly American English departments where study of Native literatures is still spotty at best, but it does very little to mend the contemporary problems of today's Native nations.

Contemporary indigenous issues are not necessarily better addressed in the sociology department, but contemporary problems from the legacy of colonization can and must be addressed in non-western ways through the legacy of life our Native ancestors have left us in their auto/biographies. Now it is long overdue to make from them what the ancestors intended for their stories: to speak to their descendents in a western cultural way that transmits Native American cultural knowledge and traditional experience. No matter the

American people's race, ethnicity, or religion, we are all now children living on the bounty of Turtle Island. We eat Her food, drink Her water, and breathe Her air every day, no matter how we identify ourselves ethnically and despite our political beliefs. We need the wisdom of the Native elders whose spirits remain here, and who are stronger than ever, in order to flourish. In the following paragraphs is a discussion containing ways of listening and reporting what one hears from the Native American auto/biographical past, present, and future. Analyzing methodology also helps to conceptualize the traits Indigenous Communal Narrative possesses, and why they are important. Cultural differences in the perceptions of women is another key characteristic to understand barriers present in the genre.

Research practices are the ways researchers gather, process, and interpret their findings; and theoretical and critical study of research practices is called methodology. Research methodology is the study of research practices (DeVault 31); for example, evaluating and studying the types of questions asked of research subjects, how the questions are asked, and how the researcher interprets the answers is research methodology. Though researchers' personal beliefs influence their research, it is still considered unbiased, made public, and becomes academic doctrine, social policy, and public law. This reality speaks to the enormous power academic writing holds over human beings and all beings, and necessitates its ethical collection and reporting. For example, what researchers and scientists say is true about the effects of fossil fuel use on our natural environment is taken into consideration by elected officials when laws are created, or dismantled, to affect the environment for good or ill.

Social scientist Shulamit Reinharz suggests that researchers redefine objectivity, away from trying to eliminate all personal influences on our research and toward a clear understanding of their influence on it (*On Becoming*...255). In other words, there is no scientific objectivity, which western cultural sciences are founded on. Who we are as researchers affects the research itself. Reinharz rightly asserts that "subjectivity can reflect the deepest possible connection between the individual thinker (researcher) and the world" (243). The deepest possible connection to which she refers I would characterize as the transformative outcome of the research process: Both the researcher and the subjects gain something significant from their interaction. Objectivity is divisive, and not traditionally Native, because separation that is devoid of emotional and spiritual connection is its goal between researcher and research subjects. How the researcher defines her or himself (by class, sex, race, and so on) are fixed components in the experiment and information gathering process. I would completely eliminate the notion and goal of objectivity altogether, as it is unattainable and irrelevant to the study of indigenous cultures. DeVault argues that "multiple versions of truth" is sought, rather than one, researcher defined truth or science defined narrative ("Talking Back..."41). The richness of collective voices, or communal truths, are sought rather than the so-called truth of individuals (44). This approach is an attempt at wholeness, though a singular voice can at times certainly illuminate the experiences of the whole. This is the foundational notion behind Indigenous Communal Narrative. Attention to respect for the speaker, acceptance of her or his testimony, responsibility to the research subject and her or his community, a call for social change, and a transformation of the academic disciplines all play a role in unbiased research methodology. These characteristics are quite similar to the objectives of those defining Native American ways of knowing.

Responsibility to the research subject means the university student or professor goes to a Native community after gaining permission from its leaders, gathers information, and then ensures that information benefits the Native community, not just the researchers' personal careers. Ways information gathering might benefit a Native community are public disclosure of injustice in United States governing practices with Native peoples, environmental pollution on reservation lands, discrimination in local schools against Native children, discrimination against unenrolled Natives, and so on. The research should seek justice after gathering information by ensuring her or his findings are made public. The research may also engage in a letter writing campaign to local non-Native elected officials who can use their influence to correct the problem. These are only a few examples of what researcher responsibility means.

Barbara Mann discusses in her book *Native Americans, Archaeologists, and the Mounds* the primary flaw of most academic study of Native peoples. She notes that the problem still persists today: the refusal of most researchers to accept Native testimonials as central (103–110). It was not that long ago that the testimony of African Americans and women in a court of law was patently suspect and often held inadmissible, most especially when the testimony was given against a white male. Such refusal to accept Native cultural testimony as valid, an ethnocentric practice, occurs across the disciplines: from science to the social sciences and humanities. Native peoples are not seen as reliable sources for the history, cosmology, culture, creation, and overall ethnic studies of themselves. This attitude is repeated by most ethnographers who wrote the Native American autobiographies around 1900 and before. Even in our current age, Native American scholars are routinely dismissed as being biased researchers and writers when presenting analysis and research in Native American Studies. No one in academia routinely claims that the writers of *The New York Times* or *The New Yorker* are culturally biased because many of them live in New York City and are EuroAmerican. Furthermore, EuroAmerican male professors are not routinely, if ever, condemned for their inability to be "fair and objective" when teaching the works of the white, male author William Shakespeare. These illustrations demonstrate the blatant racism inherent in the "all Native American researchers, professors, and their publications are biased" argument that is still routinely used against indigenous academics today. This was, and often still is, a common argument used against African American scholars in the past. The premise is that only EuroAmerican observations, research, and writing are valid and worthy of study and publication, and Native Americans', among others, are not. Native testimony was and still is perceived as inaccurate because it is not based on premises held by EuroAmerican researchers, as scholar Vine Deloria, Jr., discusses in *Red Earth, White Lies*. The practice of Native oral transmission, communal knowledge, and cosmologies quite different from the EuroAmericans' have been characterized as primitive, unscientific, and therefore unreliable for scientific inquiry (49).

Deloria notes some significant differences between Native American and EuroAmericans' beliefs about knowledge and how it is gained. They include understanding that knowledge is personal for Natives, in contrast to science where "everyone can know"; Natives believe knowledge is given through particular mediums/creatures (animals, plants, stars) to a person who is especially able to learn of it; EuroAmerican researchers conduct research to promote themselves and their discipline; Native Keepers had/have nothing to gain by altering information; and last, Natives see the earth as a living being; EuroAmericans see the physical world as an "it" (52–57). Considering the enormity of these differences, the utmost care must be taken when reworking or creating a work about a traditional Native American from the past or present. The task really should be undertaken by culturally identified researchers because the challenges to maintain cultural insight and authenticity are so great.

Another barrier in the Native American studies discipline is the distribution of information. Mann describes the distribution of information in the western linear model as radically different from the Native one. The western model sees information and opinions "scattered along a line" thus creating extreme and neutral points of view ("Euro-Forming the Data" 185). To the contrary, the Native model is a system of "interlocking ideas [that] may be arrived at via any number of routes through the web, similar to the way information is accessed on the Internet" (185). This model is circular, and it relies upon the practice of communal ethics and thus the inclusion of all points of view for the perpetuation of the community (185). She continues by noting that the context in which information is conveyed in Native culture is part of the information and that when ethnographers remove bits of information from the entire scenario that it was conveyed, meaning is lost and distorted (185). What this essentially means is that when an ethnographer excludes information about a Native subject's community and cultural system, the meaning of the subject's life and the identity of the person herself and her nation, is wrongly transmitted.

When conducting research and analyzing observations and information about Native American peoples and their writing and culture, researchers need to consider the following core themes and distinctions discussed by Walter Capps in *Seeing with a Native Eye*: Time has no past or future, but is in the "perennial reality of the now"; Natives work from a "sacred center" and space is not something to conquer or possess; Nothing exists in isolation, but all life is connected and interrelated" (28–34). Researchers should not compartmentalize their research experience by keeping two worlds distinct (35). Similar to what Reinharz argues for, the researcher should seek to connect in authentic ways with her or his subjects for dynamic and insightful research results.

At its core, Native American methodology is a belief in practicing respect and acceptance in research of the cultural beliefs of groups and individuals without discounting or evaluating their beliefs based on the researcher's cultural background. It strongly values the research subject's community benefiting from the research. As Linda Tuhiwai Smith notes in her widely read book *Decolonizing Methodologies: Research and Indigenous People*, academic research is usually utterly worthless to Natives because it does not stop them from dying or help them economically (4). On the contrary, works of Indigenous Communal Narrative do exactly the opposite: They support the perpetuation of the lives and communities of indigenous nations via authentic cultural reporting about First Nations peoples and history, and therefore shine light on their contemporary struggles. Ultimately, they are a demand for justice and social equity, which are the founding principles of the United States government that were modeled from the Eastern Woodlands nations and practiced for millennia before the settlers arrived. It is time everyone benefits from these principles once again.

How contemporary writers, ethnographers, and historians might apply these methodologies to create Indigenous Communal Narrative and re-create Native American Autobiographies already in print should become clearer. First of all, the writer would need to possess, or better yet be closely engaged with, cultural knowledge of the individual subject's nation, i.e., the best writer for this task is a Native person who has had a lifetime of experiential knowledge in her or his own culture. This would improve the chances that Native methodology is presented in the final product. If writers are non-Native persons, they will need to possess the ability to let go of the notion that their culture is central and all others are illegitimate or of unequal worth. In other words, they will have to de-center themselves and center the ethics and values of the Native nation they are writing about. The writers of any ethnicity would need to understand the process of how one respectfully gains traditional information, if one is permitted to have access to it at all. Washing dishes and carrying wood for elders, after permission from the Tribal Council to speak to those elders is gained, is the usual method. Another significant obstacle may be actually finding off-reservation Native Americans, since over half of the indigenous North American population does not live on a reservation. The writers would need to be willing to do this (yes, wash dishes and carry wood). They will need to think culturally about and conceptualize life culturally, as the subject did; being born to the subject's nation and raised in its cultural traditions will significantly improve the chances that the work will accurately represent that Native person.

Second, collaborating with other Native writers of Indigenous Communal Narrative, or Native writers and academics in general, would be a significant benefit to those who wish to revise the autobiographies in this genre. Gaining direction, guidance, and approval from elders within the institution called academia would make the final product stronger and would also model communal ethics by its very production process. The elders in academia will be able to steer newcomers away from texts that, though they are routinely purchased and used in the college classroom and cited in faculty's research, are Eurocentric and deeply flawed.

Third, writers will most necessarily need to believe that the creation story and religious beliefs of the Native person they are writing about are true—yes, true. If the writer holds the ethnocentric belief that the creation story of the Native subject's nation is just her or his belief, meaning true for them but not True, then the work will certainly be written from the position of an outsider and an authentic communal narrative will be impossible. The writer, or reviser of an already published Native autobiography, must believe in the religious suppositions of the nation she or he is writing about. This is not at all to suggest that the writer needs to be exclusively or singularly of that belief system (that is western culture, remember!). However, I am arguing that the writer must believe in the legitimacy and validity of the systems about which she or he is writing. Perceiving an indigenous nation's creation story as merely information about a belief system will create a hollow final product: the dis-belief, and consequently the subjectification of the Native person, will always be there lurking behind the text and rendering a flawed, colonized book. This is the foundation from which all communal narratives are written, and in order to ensure authenticity, there must be a belief in the truth of the creation story. If some writers/ethnographers find this requirement too much to accept, then they should find another line of work.

These are some examples of what writing an Indigenous Communal Narrative and revising a work of Native American autobiography might entail. Stepping out of western cultural modes of thinking, researching, and writing while simultaneously engaging in thinking, researching, and writing in the Native cultural tradition is essential.

Sample Discussion of an Indigenous Communal Narrative: *Mourning Dove: A Salishan Autobiography*

The 1990 work of Jay Miller entitled *Mourning Dove: A Salishan Autobiography* is a premier example of taking auto/biographical information of a Native American from the 1800s and creating an Indigenous Communal Narrative. Miller used Mourning Dove's own autobiographical writing to construct the book. At the time of his writing and research for the book, Miller was a fellow and editor/assistant director of the D'Arcy McNickle Center for the History of the American Indian (Introduction X). He explains in the introduction his substantive experience with Elders of the Colville (his subject's nation) and his close relationship, both personal and academic, with the Colville Nation. He offers details about how he came about viewing, possessing, and analyzing Mourning Dove's writings, and then how he proceeded to translate and edit them. This information is in the book's introduction, where it should be. Colville Elders were consulted at length for the book's creation, and Miller is clearly an academic and traditional scholar on Colville culture and history.

This impressive and definitive work on Salish writer Mourning Dove (1888–1936) serves as an exemplary model for all Indigenous Communal Narratives yet to be created. Miller has engaged in precisely the task I am suggesting for the proper use of the auto/biographical materials available today about indigenous peoples of the past. In the introduction the author reveals his sources of the auto/biographical materials of the indigenous subject and is clear about how editing was completed. The primary text consists of the indigenous subject's testimony/writing, and this is presented in a way that expresses indigenous communal culture. Miller explicitly notes this in the introduction: that auto/biographical books about an indigenous person must reflect communal perspective and ethos. He also offers a few paragraphs that serve as a brief, but important, lesson about Native American autobiography and how it differs from auto/biography of non-indigenous or western culture peoples. This information is appropriate and important to include because a first-time reader of such a text would most likely not realize there are differences between the two forms.

The heart of the book is Mourning Dove's writing that is organized by sections titled: A Woman's World, Seasonal Activities, and Okanogan History. Within these sections are several essays on a variety of topics that reveal the life of the subject and of her nation. Daily life, ritual, schooling, tribal ceremonies, and the stations of a human life are discussed in detail that only simultaneously reinforce to the reader the writer's sense of self and how that self is an integral part of her nation. That one does and cannot exist without or outside of the other is evident. What this means is that Mourning Dove's writing maintains a traditional perspective and that her cultural perspective was not erased or debased by the editor.

Next, Miller offers extensive endnotes with culture specific elaboration on points from Mourning Dove's text on Colville culture, language, tradition, customs, and understanding of gender, and changes that occurred to these cultural notions in Mourning Dove's, and even modern, times. In these notes, Miller offers many sources for readers' continued education in Colville history and culture, as well as sources of his information. He demonstrates the depth of his understanding of indigenous culture by clearly noting Colville, and most Native, cultural perspectives like, "The female sphere was unto itself, as was the male sphere. In this separation, Native people see cooperation and complementarity rather than antagonism" (208). This statement illustrates his ability to see and comprehend beyond American/western cultural beliefs and therefore is an important indication that his commentary is not culturally biased and consequently inaccurate. In addition to this, he expresses cultural sensitivity to the hardships brought to the Colville peoples by colonization. Most importantly, he demonstrates reverence for elders and honors their testimony as valid contributions to the collaborative effort he undertook in writing the book.

After the endnotes section, which spans forty pages, there is a Glossary of Colville-Okanogan Terms. Included in this portion of the book are all Native words used in Mourning Dove's writing with translations and comments. There is also included "transliterations into present day standard Colville-Okanogan orthography" (235), which Miller clearly understands. In this section, he recognizes the individuals with whom he collaborated for this information. What Miller is accomplishing with the inclusion of the glossary is a significant teaching about the Colville peoples. Ultimately, he is conveying to readers and to history that not merely Mourning Dove, the writer and subject of the book, is worthy of study but that her nation and all Native nations are worthy of study. He demonstrates by simple information that the Colville peoples had/have a complex culture, and this disqualifies the still perpetuated racist supposition that Native peoples are crude, uncivilized nations without culture, language, or advanced human systems of philosophy, governance, and spirituality. By merely including the glossary, Miller makes a powerful statement about the Colville peoples that is impossible to ignore and is a vehicle to speaking to the racism of the past and dissipating the racism of today.

Last in the book are Miller's references, which show the expansive research he conducted and the clear trail he traveled to create the finest possible work on Grandmother Mourning Dove. To have available to the public similar work on all indigenous elders who offered testimony in the past about their people and their own lives would create a library of Native American culture and history of unparalleled richness.

❋ CHAPTER THREE
Black Elk

The book *Black Elk Speaks*, published in 1932, remains one of the most famous of all the as-told-to stories in the Native American autobiographical genre. It is still widely read around the world, researched, and analyzed by academic scholars, and studied in the college classroom. (For additional literary study about the book *Black Elk Speaks*, which expands on various literary issues not appropriate to address here, see Hertha Wong's, William Powers's, Clyde Holler's, and Julian Rice's works noted in the bibliography.) The book chronicles the Lakota elder Black Elk's life stories told to ethnographer John G. Neihardt and transcribed by Neihardt's daughter, Enid. Black Elk's son, Ben, served as interpreter as Black Elk did not speak or read English. The book was conceived of and transcribed in an era of bitter racism against Native North Americans, and Neihardt clearly wished to convey a sympathetic image of the Indians. Unfortunately, he unwittingly reinforced stereotypes and denied all generations of readers of the text the necessary cultural information needed to truly know and appreciate Black Elk and Lakota history and culture.

As famous as the work is, and considering it is regarded as a primary literary mouthpiece for all Native cultures, one must ask the important question: Is it an Indigenous Communal Narrative? Only Indigenous Communal Narratives authentically reflect Native culture expressed in print in the auto/biographical genre. The Lakota scholar, Vine Deloria, Jr., writes in the book's Preface that the book has become a general representation of Native cultures. This is unfortunately true, and that fact should be challenged by re-creating the text. *Black Elk Speaks* is about Lakotas, not Native peoples in general. Their culture has little resemblance to Eastern Woodlands culture, Navajo culture, Inuit culture, or to the other thousands of indigenous cultures throughout the Americas. Though there are certainly similarities among all indigenous peoples, e.g., communal values and relationship with the earth, how those structures are practiced and envisioned and how they came about, are quite different from nation to nation. Accepting that Neihardt's book on Black Elk speaks for all indigenous peoples is accepting cultural erasure; something that is utterly unacceptable if one is committed to expunging stereotypes of Native peoples that still perpetuate racism, exclusion, and acts of hatred toward Native peoples today.

Let us now regard the criteria for an Indigenous Communal Narrative and apply it to Neihardt's work *Black Elk Speaks* from the information one can learn from the book itself. This is precisely how most college professors, college students, and the general world-readership experience the book: as a self-contained narrative about a Native American wherein one can draw conclusive cultural information about Native American nations in general. Therefore, we need to scrutinize the work closely with the question, "Does the book represent the Lakota people culturally?" Indeed, this is precisely the non-Native reader's perception: that the book is ultimately about the Lakota and all Native Americans. Of course, one can already see the answer unfolding as we begin to examine the text under the Indigenous Communal Narrative definitions.

First of all, John Neihardt's cultural background is EuroAmerican and he was an academic. His scholarship in Native American studies, as he discloses in the Preface and Appendix I, was from personal interest and contact with Native peoples of the Plains, primarily if not solely, elder Plains Indian men. He wrote a narrative poem collection titled *Cycle of the West* before he wrote *Black Elk Speaks*. He was enthralled by Native American peoples and events, especially the Indian Wars, and made acquaintances with people on the Dakota reservations. There is little information we can learn from the book about his formal education. At his time in American history there were no Native-centered teachings or courses in higher education about the Native American experience in North America. What was offered in colleges and universities was from a colonizer's point of view that

characterized Native Americans as savages, subhuman, and possessing no real culture. There was emphasis on saving the bit of humanity
within the Indians, while simultaneously destroying her or his "In-
dianness," i.e., destroying her or his non-Anglo, non-Christian self via
forced assimilation to EuroAmerican culture. Further, Neihardt appears to have also accepted the romanticized version of the Indian
popular of his times, for that is precisely the image he conveys in the
book: a person living a carefree utopian-like life existing off the earth
without laws, governance, or culture. Therefore, we can confidently
say that he had no formal education in Native cultures, and that his
perceptions were based only on personal information and, unfortunately, the stereotyped images and misinformation of the times.

Neihardt did consult Native American elders in order to gain information for his book; its subject is that one and the same person.
However, no other elders or Tribal Councils were consulted to review
the final literary product most likely because few Native elders read
in English at that time, though Ben Black Elk did attend Carlisle Indian School and read and spoke in English. Also, to perceive Native
peoples as worthy and capable of consulting to review a manuscript
for publication was unlikely. At the time, and unfortunately this still
remains true today to some degree, Native Americans were believed
to be fascinating subjects for Anglo writers, but not capable creators of
their own, western culture-style books and narratives. One reason for
this is because contemporary Native American writers, along with
their ancestors who were writers, often do not adhere to western cultural writing styles, themes, chronology, or structures as does literature in the English tradition. Thus, their work is perceived as flawed
because it is not similar to the Anglo-Saxon model.

Included in the newest edition of *Black Elk Speaks* is an Introduction written by Vine Deloria, Jr., which is an important addition adding Nation-specific commentary to the text. Still, there is no evidence
of any statement from the Lakota Nation, or Sioux Tribal Council,
about the book. Comments from them might include how the text has
impacted American cultural perceptions about Lakota peoples, if the
book is used in reservation classrooms, revisions and insights on misinformation from the text, alternative historical records and stories,

and so on. These are significant omissions. There is no glossary of Lakota terms or biographical information about people Black Elk mentions in his story or of leaders during his lifetime.

We know that the interview of Black Elk was a collaborative effort
of Black Elk speaking in Lakota to his son Ben who translated the Lakota to English. These words were then transcribed by Neihardt's
daughter Enid. From there, the editorial process began. In Appendix
III critical analysis is offered of the original transcript written by Enid
Neihardt and a comparison is made of the edited document that became the published text. As Raymond DeMallie, associate professor of
Anthropology, Indiana University, notes in the appendix, significant
changes were made from the original document to the final publication. What would be interesting to hear in the appendix is not what a
EuroAmerican anthropologist from the 1960s noted in the two documents, but what several traditional Lakota elders had to say about the
editorial cuts, the traditions Black Elk discusses in his stories, and
how the stories reflect (or not) Lakota culture. This could be a significant addition to the text, and deeply enrich what Black Elk shared
about his life and his nation's history. Most importantly, inclusion of
such commentary would demonstrate Native American cultural philosophy and values.

There are many published scholarly discussions about these topics
concerning Neihardt's work with Black Elk; however, they do not appear within the book. This is a key point. Because they are not included in the book, it continues to stand alone offering its monologue
about Lakota culture from an outsider's point of view, which is unacceptable because the monologue it offers does not represent Lakota,
or any Native, culture. Most college instructors who desire to teach
Native American literatures and religions, along with the average
consumer walking into any American or European bookstore, do not
have sufficient Native cultural knowledge or have completed appropriate research to make informed evaluations of this text. This is precisely the problem in allowing the book to continue to speak for itself
about Native cultures.

Deloria writes, "It is now common knowledge among scholars in
the discipline that Neihardt admittedly changed for effect many parts

of Black Elk's story, and that the editors of the book changed even more parts of it" (Neihardt xiv). Black Elk did not review the proof copy of the book and send his suggestions back to the editor. Neihardt did that. Only a reader who is familiar with Native American cultures in general, Lakota beliefs in particular, the life of Black Elk, and the imperialist United States history in North America might differentiate what is Native in the book from what is European. Few who are readers, even enthusiasts, of the book are learned in these areas, however. Therefore, discerning what is Native from what is western culture is impossible for them.

We have from this text commentary from only one indigenous person: Deloria, and that is unfortunate. Despite the respect Deloria commanded in both Native communities and in academia, more discussion is necessary from the community of Native scholars and Lakota community members. This would give readers a broader sense of what Native people are saying about the work. They might be included in an additional appendix, but an entire new edition of the book would offer the type of comprehensive background I am suggesting is necessary.

Whether the work *Black Elk Speaks* reflects the cultural philosophy of the subject's Native nation is a point discussed at length over several decades by many literary critics and scholars of Native American studies. Their words are not included with the text, however. It is commonly noted that the conceptualization, expression, methodology, and cultural values and beliefs expressed within the text are not representative of Native American culture. For example, Neihardt gave Black Elk's story an ending; this is a western literary technique Arnold Krupat, among others, discusses. Native Americans see life as evolving and ongoing, but Neihardt's rendering of Black Elk's story does not demonstrate that central belief (*For Those Who*...130). Further, Neihardt and his editors changed whatever portions of Black Elk's stories they wished, just as Krupat has noted about the ending. From the Preface: "...some scholars have said that the book reflects more of Neihardt than it does of Black Elk..." (xiv). Krupat himself observes that "Neihardt rewrote much of Black Elk's accounts and gave them an 'ending,' which is a Christian, western approach to the medicine man's life which, to him, was still evolving and growing, not at an end as Neihardt's story asserts" (*For Those Who*...130).

Native cultures value communal beliefs. For example, Neihardt noted that Black Elk's sacred vision from childhood had begun to make him ill (161). When Black Elk told an elder about his vision, the elder said he must tell his story, through performance, to the people so he could be free of the illness. Black Elk explains later, on page 204, how the story belongs to the people; that Black Elk was given the vision, not for himself, but for the people. However, because the book is written in the western literary style, it implies that Black Elk was the originator of the vision and the story, that it remains his story (Black Elk speaks, not the Lakota Nation speaks), that he was somehow remarkable for receiving the story, and therefore through the book his individuality is emphasized. This way of understanding a Native autobiographical text is a western cultural construct that disregards communal philosophy and thereby produces an inaccurate portrayal of Black Elk, his Lakota nation, and Native Americans in general.

Though the subject of Native American autobiographical books like *Black Elk Speaks* is the Native American individual, how Black Elk's stories are presented by Neihardt are European and not representative of Native culture. An Indigenous Communal Narrative can feature a single Native American person and still be representative of the individual's community.

The key difference between a Native American autobiography and an indigenous communal narrative is that in an Indigenous Communal Narrative the Native American individual's community is also included in the book so the individual Native person does not stand alone offering a personal monologue in the Puritan sermon format of one speaker speaking for all in unrelenting, linear order. The absence of voices from Black Elk's community is a serious problem. This is a key characteristic denoting Native culture, which is communal, and which differs from EuroAmerican culture which is individual centered. The writer of the story (Neihardt) manipulates Black Elk's stories in a way that renders them European with a Native theme.

There is a great silence in this book from important members of Black Elk's community: the leaders of the Lakota (chiefs, tribal councils, and clan mothers) and the story keepers, including the voices of pivotal EuroAmerican settlers and Indian Agents, animals, trees, rivers, and the earth. Further, there are no stories at all from the Lakota women. Indeed, there is only made central one man (Black Elk) and a few of his friends with the ever-present shadow of Neihardt's editorial pen over all involved. Nearly all of Black Elk's community is missing from the book so that it nearly mirrors the type of autobiography that Daniel Boone might have written. There is of course nothing at all culturally inappropriate with the autobiographical style someone like Daniel Boone might have employed; however, this style is simply not at all appropriate for autobiographies or biographies of indigenous peoples. A significant difference between Black Elk's words and the writing of Boone would be that Boone would have final say on what was written in his own autobiography, whereas Black Elk did not. Perhaps *Black Elk Speaks* has become so popular among contemporary Americans and Europeans because it clearly models the western culture literary style of the bragging male hero speaking of battles and glory.

In relation to the battles, it is important to note that Black Elk's words ultimately represent "all Indians" to contemporary readers, and the Lakota-EuroAmerican battles he conveys are lost by the Lakota. One chapter is even quite gruesomely, and appropriately, titled "The Butchering at Wounded Knee." These stories only reinforce the stereotype of Indians as helpless victims who are doomed because they not only lost these wars, but lost all their culture. This is a western cultural way of understanding a nation of people: that only the result of war is significant. It is the belief that the results of war are the sole pivotal historic experiences of a people, and are the sum total and defining representation of a people. This rendition is simply not Native cultural thinking. This observation is not meant at all to diminish the importance of Black Elk and his friends relaying what happened to the Lakota in pivotal EuroAmerican conquest battles. To the contrary, readers simply do not hear enough of what was happening in their community among all peoples during these intense and dark times for the Native peoples of the Plains. For example, how were the Lakota's hunting grounds affected by colonization? How was their governing system affected. Did it remain intact? What happened to the women and children? There are many more defining aspects of a nation of people beyond the outcomes of war and the battles themselves. In order to understand the Lakota's communal experiences, readers need to know more. It was Neihardt's responsibility to see that those stories were added to Black Elk's stories so that a product of Indigenous Communal Narrative might be created. Unfortunately, Black Elk's community is utterly missing from this so-called autobiography, and this is the principle reason that Neihardt's work cannot, by any means, be categorized as an Indigenous Communal Narrative.

In relation to Native and colonial contact, the work tells of Native and EuroAmerican contact specifically in relation to warfare between the two groups. This is an important feature of the text because little documentation of those Native Americans actually participating, even surviving, battles against the EuroAmericans is available in terms of how much documentation there is available about the EuroAmericans' experience in these battles. Black Elk tells Neihardt stories from the Battle of Wounded Knee, among others, that show the injustice and tragedy of Lakota and colonial contact. An important addition Neihardt might have made, and re-creators of the text today could make, is including important information about Native and EuroAmerican contact other than military battles. For example, laws governing religious freedom on the reservation, land use, jobs, education, trade, and change in Lakota traditions in this time period would be interesting and important additions in an endnotes section to future reissues of the book. This would offer readers a more complex understanding of what colonization did to the Lakota specifically, and how they survived, rather than the dismal, hopeless picture *Black Elk Speaks* creates and perpetuates about Native peoples being utterly destroyed in general.

The creation story of the Lakota is missing from the text. This is a serious problem because without this information, we cannot understand the Lakota culture. Without understanding the Lakota culture we cannot understand Black Elk or his story: each reflect the other.

The story of how the Sacred Pipe was brought to the Lakota people is included in the first chapter. Though it is one of the most important and sacred teachings of the Lakota, parts of the version Black Elk supposedly told are suspect. For example, on page 3, one of the scouts in "The Offering of the Pipe" story is said to have "had bad thoughts and spoke them" because the bringer of the pipe was a woman. This is pure western cultural thinking that created and condones sexualization of women. Indigenous cultures did not represent women based on their sexual status or behavior (in terms of never had sex, has had sex, has had sex with one or multiple partners, and so on). These notions were brought to Turtle Island by Europeans; priests of European religions to be exact. There are also word choices such as "behold" and "you shall multiply" and references to "good" people and "bad" people. These words characterize western religious beliefs, are not present or conceptualized in traditional Native cultures in this way, and would certainly not have come from a traditional Native elder unless he was Christianized. Perhaps this is Neihardt's editorial hand once again, but we cannot know from the text alone. Here again contemporary Native scholars' commentary would add authenticity to these passages and clarify the culturally nebulous points that certainly require clarification to reveal fully Lakota culture of Black Elk's era. The Native scholar would of course need to be mindful of not obscuring Lakota culture with her or his own colonized point of view.

In terms of Neihardt's understanding of the relationship Native people have with the earth and all other non-human beings, that information is discreetly conveyed through the voice of Black Elk. Though Black Elk apparently referred to the months of the year in traditional Lakota terms, is named after an animal (a member of his community), and speaks of Earth and Her creatures in respectful ways, it is not clear that Neihardt is convinced that these other beings are legitimate members of a community. None of their voices are present in the book similar to how those few human voices are present. This is a somewhat deficient area in the book, but what is included in the stories is how certain animals affected Black Elk's life and played a significant role in his sacred vision. This is important information that conveys Native cultural beliefs; however, Neihardt's lack of firsthand experiential knowledge of communities other than the human one is present in the book: the absence is present. For example, we hear throughout the book about Black Elk's experiences with animals, plants, and spirits, but our writer and silent but powerful editor (Neihardt) is never engaged in those experiences and thus a type of hollowness or illegitimacy is conveyed. In other words, it seems legitimate that the "wild" Indian can wear feathers and talk with spirits, but the "civilized" EuroAmerican (always pictured in a suit) is on the outside watching the performance. This is still a popular perspective in contemporary American times: it is acceptable for non-Natives to go to a pow-wow to be entertained with Native dancing and prayers, but it is understood culturally that "spiritual stuff" is for Indians, not civilized EuroAmerican people who are either modernized or Christianized and are too sophisticated to commune with non-human beings. For example, on page 271 at the conclusion of the book, Neihardt writes, "What happened is, of course, related to Wasichu readers as being merely a more or less striking coincidence." He refers to an experience with Black Elk and the Thunder Beings' response to his praying at a sacred place. Again, Neihardt seems to be asking the reader: Is it Indian Spiritual Theater or real, i.e., "real" to non-Native people? He does not convince the reader that he believes it is real or anything more than a fascination. However, the true Indigenous Communal Narrative leaves no room for speculation on this point. The chronicler/writer will come across as being a member of that community that she or he writes about and conveys cultural authenticity in every word. There is no Indian Spiritual Theater; rather, readers are convinced of the legitimacy of the Native cultural beliefs and that the chronicler believes them, too.

What of the social, economic, cosmologic, and political structures of the subject's nation? Readers can garner very little information about these categories from the book, which is a serious deficiency. We learn bits of information throughout Black Elk's story, as if it was the custom for him to protect his deceased cousin's wife, but why? From where did that custom come? Is this about gender or clan lineage? Is this part of the teaching stories of his people? Part of the creation story? We are never told. Black Elk says the women came on to the battlefield singing their tremolo, but what is their role in relation to war? To prisoners? Again, we are not told, yet readers should know this. The absence of the structures of Lakota culture means we really only learn a bit about Black Elk, little to nothing of his people, and, therefore, western cultural ways of knowing and transmitting information are reinforced. This is a long way of saying that cultural erasure is perpetuated because of the absence of cultural knowledge in the Native auto/biographical genre. What the reader experiences is a Native man wearing a European story, and this simply cannot be admitted into the worldwide literary record as being an authentic Native text because it is not. Only Indigenous Communal Narratives are. *Black Elk Speaks* falls far from acceptable in that measurement.

In terms of information about gender, Neihardt's book is a great offender in this literary genre. Grandmothers, Grandmother Spirits, and Grandmother Leadership are never noted, and their absence clearly states that they did not exist. This is especially so because women's spiritual presence and leadership are routinely not mentioned, or not acknowledged, in religious texts of western culture. In other words, because it is commonplace to see God as male and key religious figures as male in western culture, it would be easy for an American reader to simply assume that Lakota deities are all male as well. From what we learn from Black Elk's autobiography, it seems Lakota women only appear to sing the tremolo after the men did something great, for that is the only information Neihardt offers the reader. This is indeed characteristic of western cultural literary works, which historically feature only men and the experiences of men; however, there is most certainly an additional reason for the absence of women's stories which readers could not possibly surmise: same-gendered protocols.

Black Elk could not speak about the matters, roles, customs, experiences or duties of the women because, first, he is male; second, he is speaking to a man (Neihardt); and third, he would have little knowledge of women's culture because he was barred from knowing it. Same-gendered speakership means that women relayed and maintained the matters of the women to other women, not to men, and that men spoke with and shared their stories with men. Even if Black Elk was familiar with the experiences of the Lakota women, it would be inappropriate for him to discuss them because he is a man, and it would be even more cultural folly to discuss them with Neihardt, who was also a man. Women have the privilege of discussing their own experiences and traditions with each other (most often appropriate to clan membership), and women would share the matters of the women with a woman ethnographer, if they wished. Neihardt probably did not know about this important information, but with the appropriate questions, he could have easily discovered it. Indeed, he could have employed the help of his daughter and added significant information from the women's lodge about life during this era. Adding this information now would be quite useful to readers and would further reveal Lakota tradition and a tradition that is common to many Native cultures (same-gendered protocols).

Unfortunately, the absence of women's voices and the absence of noting the same-gendered speakership point reinforce western cultural expectations that women should be omitted from the historic record. In addition, it also reinforces that what women did was not as important as the men's actions, and western cultural readers would naturally just assume this because western culture makes absent women from the historic record and routinely diminishes women's contributions to our world. Therefore, it seems only "natural" that women themselves and women's contributions to Black Elk's life and the Lakota nation are absent from the book. Natural, that is, to a reader from western culture who is accustomed to women being absent from literary and historic works overall.

The discussion just offered would appear to an academic as a feminist reading of the text, but that is a western cultural construction or way of thinking. Feminism is a western construct that does not illumine gendering. Feminism is academic; gendering is spiritual, a conscious replication and re-enactment of the balanced halves of the cosmos. Any resemblance between western feminism and Native gendering is superficial. They are culturally based institutions, grounded in distinct analyses of reality that have nothing in common. The absence of women in *Black Elk Speaks* is purely cultural: western culture. My observation of their absence is also based in cultural perspective: indigenous culture. If the work was a true Indigenous Communal Narrative, that is reflecting Native culture, the voices of the women in Black Elk's life would be revealed and allowed to speak for themselves, or the editor would be quite clear that this is solely the men's version of parts of Lakota culture. This is the only way to create a community of voices and thus a cultural replication of the times so that we in the future might gain authentic Lakota cultural knowledge from the era of Black Elk's life.

To add to the problems of gender in the book, Neihardt, and even Black Elk, convey images of women that are utterly non-Native. Not only are women absent from the text, but they are referred to in the diminishing ways that western culture routinely refers to them. In almost all of Black Elk's stories where women are mentioned, the intrusion of western cultural interpretation is present. For example, on page 96 where the Sun Dance ceremony is described, Black Elk supposedly used the term "young maidens" and said these young maidens "had to be so good that nobody there could say anything against them, or that any man had ever known them." This is either solely Neihardt's words or perhaps came from Black Elk's European-assimilated mind because all these terms and phrases signify western cultural beliefs about women that Native cultures simply did not possess. The perceptions expressed are explicit about sexual beliefs concerning women's "purity" and women's value based on their sexual possession by men and are, therefore, entirely European. Black Elk refers to women often as virgins and maidens. These are obvious red flags for any Native-centered researcher to recognize as European-formulated thinking, but how would the general reader know this information? Alternatively, for that matter, how would a college professor know it if her or his primary scholarship most certainly is not in Native American studies, and what she or he has read is most likely culturally biased and inaccurate? One sees the enormity of the challenge for culturally analyzing the text as it is presented, that is, without help from other informed sources.

Other omissions include characters from the chapter titled "The Bison Hunt." We hear about a crier and advisers giving directions to the people, but we are never told who they are, what their roles are in the nation, if they are elected, if they are chosen, and if so by whom? Are they men and women; is gender a concern for these duties? Knowing this information matters more than for simple cultural or anthropological records. Knowing this information demonstrates to readers that the Lakota people deserve cultural respect through the acknowledgment that they possessed a legitimate culture. Omission of these cultural details perpetuates inaccurate images of the Lakota, and all Native nations, suggests that they were primitive, without their own government, social structure, and cosmology, and were culturally primitive peoples who just tried to survive from one season to the next. Without details about the Lakota culture and their experiences during this era, the fact that they were/are a wise and complexly structured nation, within the larger complex indigenous civilizations across the continent, is lost. This is an enormous missed opportunity on Neihardt's part, and for the publishers of newer editions of the book. Elaboration on these governing roles in traditional Lakota social structures could significantly change representations of them in contemporary times and also enrich Black Elk's story. Black Elk mentions the soldier band, the hunters, and the head man, but again we are not told who they are to the people, how they achieved their status, nor how this system was created. Again, this information is important because it legitimizes to the reader the complexity of the Lakota nation and would demonstrate the richness of its culture. It is difficult to stereotype and condemn a people who are perceived and acknowledged as possessing human dignity and cultural beauty. This is the role Neihardt's book could have played in our modern world, but alas, it has only cast out a few crumbs of Lakota culture to represent the whole.

Black Elk Speaks is a EuroAmerican man's book, which is unfortunate. Its popularity may be accounted for by its similarity to the western cultural literary style for autobiographical writing. It features stories about spirits, hunting, battles, and men sitting around a campfire talking about the "good old days" when they were young and brave. The book is written in chronological order (a western literary technique) and expresses beliefs that a man's best days are when he is young, and old age somehow renders him inadequate and failing.

This theme is characterized in the last pages of the book. These are not Native beliefs about the events of a person's life or their relevant ordering. Native traditional beliefs see human old age as a time of great wisdom warranting respect, dignity, and personal power (spiritual and governing), images not conveyed in the book. Further, the absence of a more authentic and complete representation of Native life through the stories and eyes of Black Elk renders the work highly flawed both as an emblem of Lakota culture and a work of communal narrative. The work misses the important opportunity of being a teaching tool to reach out to the wider EuroAmerican world, and it is a world that is still quite interested in Black Elk and things Native American. With important additions to the text, either through additional appendixes or the incorporation of the text as it is among many more chapters, *Black Elk Speaks* might become the teaching tool to change many misrepresentations still flourishing about Native peoples today and well into the future.

As we will see in Maurice Kenny's work on Tekonwatonti in chapter six, community representation greatly enriches the authentic transmission of indigenous cultures in printed form. The task is not only valuable but possible. Neihardt's work on Black Elk could serve as a springboard for a new comprehensive book that gives, not only college students, but a worldwide readership the lesson in Native American cultures they obviously still crave.

✖ CHAPTER FOUR
Pretty-shield

Ethnographer Frank B. Linderman met in Montana with the Crow Medicine Woman, Pretty-shield, and her interpreter, Goes-together, and recorded some of her life stories. Pretty-shield used sign language to speak to Linderman while Goes-together translated Pretty-shield's Crow language into English, which was then written on paper by Linderman. Linderman first published the chronicle of Pretty-shield in 1932 by the title *Red Mother*, and her thumbprint appears inside the title page under a declaration that she endorses the stories in the book. The book itself is dedicated to her granddaughter, Sarah Jane Waller. Pulling the book off the bookstore or library shelf, this is what readers will find, but what are they taught about Crow culture and Native North Americans by this book?

Unlike the appendixes and preface of *Black Elk Speaks*, readers have no way of knowing if or how much of Pretty-shield's story Linderman altered, edited, or omitted. As has been already noted, contemporary scholars and writers over the decades have added appendixes and commentary to John Neihardt's original text that clearly demonstrate the extent to which he changed Black Elk's words. This is important information and readers should have a similar sense of how much was changed of Pretty-shield's story. Unfortunately, though, we do not know this from what is written in these pages of the original 1932 text. Pretty-shield seems eager to tell her story to Linderman and makes this clear at several points throughout the book, though her reasons are not articulated. She is paid for her stories, but that hardly seems her primary motivation. She refers to the "stories of the men" and to the business of the men that she had no knowledge of because she is a woman, so same-gendered speaking seems to have a role in Crow culture just as it does in the Eastern Woodlands. We do not, however, learn explicitly about this custom in the original text.

The foreword to the book is revealing, not of Pretty-shield, but of Linderman. He often refers to his lack of experience with "old Indian women" and dubs them "diffident, and so self-effacing that acquaintance with them is next to impossible" (9). He laments that they remain "strangers" to him despite some experience he has had with Native women working as his interpreters. Unfortunately, he must have never considered asking a Crow elder man about gendered protocol for human interaction, ethnocentrically assuming that there was none in Crow culture because there is none in western culture. He could never have guessed then that those so-called "old Indian women" were not diffident and self-effacing, but were following the norms of their traditional culture based on gender. I wonder if he referred to his elder aunts, grandmothers, and women friends and colleagues as "old white women?"

Continuing in the foreword, Linderman refers to Pretty-shield's traditional stories in debasing ways by saying they were "obviously tribal myths" and "grandmother tales," which he dismisses by adding "to the Indian mind teach needed truths" (11). In the same paragraph he laments his inability to understand the dreams of "old Indians" and adds: "Trying to determine exactly where the dream begins and ends ...one cannot tell where the natural melts to meet the artificial" (11). It does not require much imagination to recognize his cultural, even gender, biases in the meager pages of the foreword. His position that traditional Crow tales are not truths, that Crow ways of knowing are not valid, and that Crow teachings cannot possibly be important to western people is obvious. Further, his western cultural perceptions of dreams and his clear lack of understanding the roles and importance of dreams in Crow culture is convoluted and alarming. Linderman clearly conveys cultural superiority right at the onset of the book, which is not a good sign for how the stories he collects will be conveyed. At the same time, he also expresses clear admiration for Pretty-shield as a caring grandmother and generous person. A reader who is accustomed to such a position of cultural superiority, one that is so often present in most written works about Native peoples, would most likely not notice it but simply accept this perception as true and appropriate. This is precisely the problem that must be rectified in order to dispel present-day stereotypes of indigenous peoples.

The book offers little information about Frank B. Linderman except that he had "much to do" with some of the Native nations in Montana over a forty-six-year period. In the appendix is a letter addressed to the "Honorable Frank B. Linderman" from Scott Leavitt, Congressman, dated 1931. The topic of the letter is about the "exact length of the lock of hair from the head of Long Hair" (254). A sacred ceremony is discussed in the letter. On the back cover of the book we learn that Linderman was born in Ohio in 1869 and was a "trapper, hunter, and cowboy" and that he was "intimately associated with the Crows and other Indian tribes." This apparently qualified him to become a chronicler of the life of a woman of a culture that he had little knowledge about, except the ins and outs of everyday life.

Considering the cultural perceptions he espouses so far in the book's foreword, readers can discern that his intimate relationship with the Crow did not alter his belief in his own culture's superiority. Intimate associations do not necessarily convey cultural knowledge of the quality that books should be made of. For example, if a cultural outsider came to the United States and lived in a small town among Americans for forty-six years, the person might still never learn of the historic events, cosmology, governing structures, or foundational belief systems that shape social power in the United States. He or she would, at best, learn of anecdotal information and garner a few representational stories. Indeed, one may rightfully argue that a random survey conducted of people in an American shopping mall would reveal that most Americans cannot successfully describe the complex governing branches of the United States, notable historic dates, or the contents of the Bill of Rights. Should they even be expected to? In other words, "intimate associates" are not valid sources for writing books that define culture for an entire nation of people! This is an immediate red flag making Linderman's work suspect of cultural erasure and distortion. As did all Native nations, there were individual Keepers of history and cultural tradition who were specifically trained to maintain, transmit, and nurture the stories and ways of their people. These are the individuals who are qualified to speak about the matters of their nation, and those stories need to then be transmitted in a written form that reinforces a Native cultural point of view.

Grandmother Pretty-shield was both an elder and a traditional medicine person. These characteristics do indeed qualify her to speak about any matters she wishes to speak of. However, just as Neihardt did with Grandfather Black Elk, Linderman has set Pretty-shield apart from her community rather than going within the community and allowing the people who are given the responsibility to represent the people to do so. This was a serious problem during the treaty making days when self-appointed, so-called Native leaders would sign contracts giving away their nation's land without the consent of the duly appointed Native leaders. I do not suggest at all that Pretty-shield erred. What I note is that there was a way of going about transmitting her stories that would have presented them within her community and therefore made them more representational of Crow cultural beliefs. That was Linderman's responsibility, but he apparently did not have the cultural education to conceptualize such a final written product. Perhaps he also could not anticipate the devastating effects the roles of negative stereotypes and ignorance played in harming Native nations, despite the prevailing racism of his era. Unfortunately, his book became one of the major contributors to the creation of the dying savage image so popular in his times and down to today.

In striking contrast to Neihardt's work about Lakota elder Black Elk, Linderman's book is rich with detailed stories about Pretty-shield's life. She discusses the particulars of not only her medicine dreams, and the dreams of others in her nation, but also describes daily tasks of the women like digging for roots, gathering berries, caring for children, playing games, putting up and taking down a lodge when the camp was moved, and so on. There are many stories of Pretty-shield's childhood that are simultaneously emotionally riveting, entertaining, and a lesson in Crow culture. Interwoven throughout the actual storytelling are bits of information about Pretty-shield's life at the time she told her stories to Linderman. Thus the work is inadvertently a statement about the devastating effects of colonization. As the Grandmother says herself, although the Lakota tormented the Crow constantly with war, they could have never imagined what the settlers were capable of. Here she referred to the sickening mass slaughter of the buffalo herds across the plains, the destruction of the Crow horse herds after colonization by EuroAmerican ranchers and farmers, and the radical reduction of their reservation lands even after treaties and contracts were signed with the new U.S. government.

The creation story of the Crow is primarily missing from this text, though there is a reference to it by Pretty-shield. She briefly refers to Old Man Coyote, Alone-Man, First Man, and First Woman or Red Woman at several points throughout the book. Little more discussion is offered than this, except one story about Red Woman. Inclusion of the creation story with Native analysis would offer readers much more information and understanding about Crow culture and beliefs, yet Linderman never pressed Pretty-shield for elaboration on these points, though he quite pointedly asked her about many other things that are traditionally private, sacred information (like "how did you get your name?"). A version of the creation story could appear in an added chapter or appendix of the book along with Crow cultural analysis. This would be an important teaching for readers with little knowledge of Crow culture.

During the many stories Pretty-shield transmitted to Linderman, he often noted that she became quite animated and expressed them dramatically through gestures, movement, and facial expressions. She might use the end of a broom or her blanket as a prop to demonstrate some aspect of her story, suddenly jump up and bear down on the table where he sat with her hands and whisper conspiratorially to him, or sing and drum with one of his pencils! These dramatizations of her stories were often so compelling that Linderman and Goes-together were startled, mesmerized, emotionally moved, or laughed uncontrollably about what Pretty-shield told and acted out for them. This is indeed Native oral performance that is the hallmark of Native storytelling! This is what contemporary Native literary analysts refer to as Native oral art or performance and is a primary argument for the rejection of writing stories down because the "life" is taken out of them. Linderman once noted that Pretty-shield made her face into the appearance of a Bear so clearly that he and Goes-together shuddered.

Pretty-shield's stories are filled with descriptions of her nation's social customs, but Linderman never asks her from where these beliefs derived. Perhaps he believed they did not derive from any cultural notion, cosmology, or belief system but were merely invented for social ease or harmony. That of course is not the case. For example, in the opening pages of the book Linderman asks Pretty-shield about how a "man treated a married sister-in-law" to which Pretty-shield replied, "Ahh, you know, or you would not have asked me" (17). She then describes this custom in the most exact of details as she was requested to do. Unfortunately, Linderman did not know to ask for elaboration on where this tradition came from, or what beliefs about gender, property, living arrangements, social interactions, and so on created it. He then asked, "And a man who married a woman had the right to demand her unmarried sisters as his wives?" (17). She replies yes to this question, which would naturally lead a reader of western culture to believe that Crow women did not have much autonomy over their own lives, especially in marriage. To the contrary, Pretty-shield notes throughout her storytelling that Crow women could refuse to marry, refuse to return to a husband whom she had left, and that the Crow were matrilineal people. For example, she tells of a widowed woman who remarries and is mistreated by the new husband: "But this man was not good to her. She left him, and died single" (34). There are other such references throughout the book. What an important opportunity was missed when Linderman did not know or care to ask the right questions concerning Crow clan structures and how those structures were originally conceived of (in the creation story, most likely). Here is where contemporary Crow scholars, elders, tribal councils, and traditional Keepers could add their knowledge to this book and tell readers so much more about their culture.

Another intriguing custom of the Crow Pretty-shield mentions in only a few sentences, and Linderman adds a few of his own lines about, is the custom of hair combing. This is seemingly a small and insignificant practice, but within this practice is important and meaningful cultural information. There is literal hair combing and then there is an additional meaning to this practice as well: unraveling and interpreting dreams. This is its meaning in the customs of the Eastern Woodlands people where women were the literal hair combers and dream translators. Pretty-shield says, "One could always tell when a man loved his woman by her hair" (33). Linderman then adds that men combed their own and their woman's hair. One must ask why and what does this mean culturally? Were Crow men the unravelers and translators of dreams? Did they carry the power of dreaming for their people? Who gave this power to them? Was this tradition transmitted to them from First Man or from Old Man Coyote? Did women ever comb hair, and what about same-sex oriented people or medicine people?

The same questions should be applied to the ritual of face painting. Pretty-shield notes that her husband first painted her face after "he had gained the right by saving a Crow warrior's life in battle" and that after this initial painting she had the right to paint her own face (131). From where did this custom originate and what does it culturally imply and demonstrate? There are always beliefs that spawn cultural traditions and those beliefs most often stem from a culture's creation story. One again sees the significant loss from its absence in this, and all Native auto/biographical, texts. The Native creation story is missing from these texts because in the western cultural literary tradition, the creation story (Genesis of the Bible) does not seem relevant in an auto/biography of a westerner. Western culture features and promotes individuals, and Native peoples centralize the community, though Native individuals certainly express pride in their merits and talents. Therefore, it never occurred to Linderman to note the Crow creation story. Most likely he did not consider it valid or worth noting anyway because of his clear cultural superiority.

Another custom that is left without commentary is lodge-cutting. Pretty-shield noted that few women cut lodges and that she knew of only one woman who painted a lodge. Lodges were painted with the medicine-dreams of their dreamers who were men, so Linderman notes. Is this true, and if so what does it mean? Pretty-shield talks often about women and their medicine dreams, medicine objects, and powerful visions and healings, so there is clearly a tradition with the women, but she does not tell of it. Throughout the book, Pretty-shield seems intent on responding precisely only to the questions she is asked. So perhaps this is why readers gain only bits of information about Crow customs: Linderman simply does not follow up with additional questions after most of her responses.

Some of the stories to which Linderman refers in the foreword as "obviously tribal myths" and "grandmother's tales" most likely include Pretty-shield's stories about the Little People or sprites, the tribe of "very large people" or giants, and the many medicine stories she shares. These stories were of course real and true happenings, but because Linderman is from a culture that does not believe or have records of certain events or experiences he unfortunately disparages them in the foreword and at times in his own commentary between her stories. For example, Pretty-shield mentions the alligator's lodge and Linderman, curious about this name because the Crow have lived in the northern Plains, explains it by saying that the Crow must have lived near the ocean at some point in their national history. He also notes that Crow storytellers often mention sea monsters as well. To a non-Native person this seems like a reasonable explanation, but upon further examination, its ethnocentric perspective is clear. Because EuroAmericans believe in the notions of science that have certain beliefs about the geographic history of North America, Linderman naturally assumes that Pretty-shield's knowledge about the alligator could not have originated in a land where science says no alligators have ever lived. More on this clash between western culture's science and indigenous cultures can be found in Deloria's *Red Earth, White Lies*. However, if Crow traditional stories were consulted, and if Pretty-shield's testimony had simply been accepted, Linderman may very well have noted that the landscape of the northern Plains did not always look the way it does now. Indeed, the far-reaching historic power of oral keepings often tell a much different story from contemporary science, and this fact should be legitimately noted.

Pretty-shield's stories come as close to being an Indigenous Communal Narrative as most of the books in this genre from this time period. Readers do not simply hear about the animals, plants, spirits, and leaders of her era, but they often speak for themselves. There is a greater sense of community and the importance of community from Pretty-shield's collective story, though Linderman does not seem to actually believe her or "get it." Despite his limits, her brilliantly conveyed stories bring to life the Crow community and their values and beliefs, though there is so much more to know. Linderman also conveys Pretty-shield's story in the western linear format (chronological order from earliest memories into the "now"), and then he leaves readers with the most grim, hopeless sense of doom for the Crow people. These means do not convey Native cultural beliefs or perceptions about life, and this is what books about Native people should convey in order to undo cultural erasure and stereotyping.

In the last pages of the book Pretty-shield talks about the significant hardships her people have endured since colonization and the Indian wars. In gruesome, heart-wrenching terms she discloses how "white men shot down our horses so that their cows and sheep might have grass" on Crow owned land. She expresses concerns about her grandchildren having to "wear out their moccasins" going to the Indian Agency office to get monies rightfully owed them. To all these lamentations, which included a prophetic statement from Pretty-shield that she had little time remaining in this world, Linderman responds with "I felt that my work was finished now" (253). A troubling, unaffected response to be sure. Was this his belief because he felt the Crow were finished as well? It seems so. Readers must wonder about his purposes for this book. Were they merely anthropologic as though his subject was a one-dimensional subject on a chart? He signs to Pretty-shield before they part that they are "friends": an odd thing to say to a revered elder with renowned medicine power! What his actions and words tell readers is that he is incapable of displacing his own cultural superiority and recognizing that talking with Grandmother Pretty-shield was a profound honor.

This chronicle of the life stories of Crow medicine woman, Pretty-shield, is a mere tip of the iceberg because it only reveals Crow life during the time Pretty-shield lived and leaves readers with the belief that Crow life ended with her life (or with colonization). By adding the Crow creation story and other important stories that shaped traditional Crow culture, discussing and explaining the clan and governing structure of the nation, and expanding on so many of the rich customs Pretty-shield raises in her stories, Linderman's text could become the exemplary teaching tool it should have been upon original publication. Linderman had the added benefit of interviewing and living among Native American speakers of their indigenous language and could have attempted to include a glossary of Crow terms, the creation of which would have been quite possible considering the fluency of Goes-together. The inclusion of such a glossary in the book would have added a level of cultural information that would have brought validation and a greater respect for Pretty-shield and Crow culture to the general public. What a world of difference such a book could have made for the Crow and other Native nations if only the Americans could listen. I believe they wish to listen now, and indeed, need to listen to Native traditional wisdom.

❧ CHAPTER FIVE
Crashing Thunder

The autobiography of Crashing Thunder, a document first published in part in 1920 and then expanded on and reissued in 1926 by ethnographer Paul Radin, is the story of a Native American of the Winnebago nation. Another reissue of the stories was published in 1999 and includes a foreword, appendix, and index by Arnold Krupat. The preface and introduction written by Radin in the early 1900s reveals his musings about the science of ethnography, American Indians, and how he acquired the story of Crashing Thunder. What we learn from him is that he wanted to learn about "real Indians" and therefore commenced field investigations in Nebraska in 1909 in order to learn of the Winnebago people (xxi). Radin was French and an academic.

Radin acquired the story of Crashing Thunder, a Winnebago man, after requests over a period of three years. When Crashing Thunder experienced "temporary poverty" he consented to write the story of his life in the Winnebago syllabary. Radin then translated Crashing Thunder's autobiography into English and eventually published it. The book is a combination of the life stories of two Winnebago men who were brothers, but Radin titles his book as though it were the autobiographical work of one person. Radin claims in the book's preface that "no changes of any kind have been introduced," which Krupat explicitly denies and demonstrates in the appendix of the most recent reissue throughout his discussion of Radin's original transcript.

Radin's preface is a monologue rehashing and adding credence to the stereotypes of Native North Americans from the 1800s unto today: that is, the nature-loving noble savage. He says that "the Indian has been a symbol for youth and freedom of expression, for freedom from the shackles of civilized constraint" and concludes that it would be "almost sacrilege to trifle with this vision" (xviiii). Within this one sentence the now schooled reader of ethnographic monographs is able to readily discern the sum total of Radin's cultural knowledge of the Winnebago and thus of Native nations in general: little to nothing. The complex, highly varied and regulated, and clearly defined cultural protocol of Native social structures is utterly missing from Radin's understanding of his subject, and this is asserted repeatedly throughout the book.

The Introduction demonstrates to readers Radin's perceived cultural position with his subject. He refers to Crashing Thunder as an "untutored savage" and a "child of nature," and offers a summary of the autobiographer's life. Radin notes that Crashing Thunder is an alcoholic "like so many people [who] seek forgetfulness in the cup" and talks about drunkenness as a generalized human ailment. He does not connect Crashing Thunder's alcoholism with colonization and the subsequent poverty and loss of cultural identity and social structures. Radin speaks often in the Introduction about psychology and human behavior formation, not mentioning, or realizing because of cultural superiority, that these are western cultural notions that have no meaning in a Native cultural context and therefore cannot amplify the events of a Native subject's life. He refers to the writings of Crashing Thunder in western literary terms and dubs the ending of the book "the most approved style of Voltaire."

In the last paragraph of the Introduction Radin expresses his desire to dispel the prevalent notions of his era, ones we hear clearly in Frank Linderman's work on Pretty-Shield, that Native people cannot discern between what is real and what is a dream, that they are incapable of being objective and presenting facts. The notions of being objective and the meaning of facts are ideas created and valued by western culture, not Native cultures. Believing that these ideas are universally important is cultural superiority. What his argument claims is that Native people have the ability to think like Europeans, meaning writing and thinking in ways that divide different ways of knowing from each other or not thinking like a Native person at all. He unfortunately cannot seem to grasp the reality that culture determines ways of knowing and expressing that knowing, and that all ways are valid and legitimate, not just the ones of western culture.

Throughout the book readers hear often about Crashing Thunder's drinking exploits, his sexual desire and attraction to women, and his belief that he is "not an ordinary being" (6). He expresses disbelief of the sacred Native ceremonies in which he participates. Radin offers some amplification of Winnebago culture in footnotes, many of which are obviously biased or only partial information. This ethnographic work raises serious questions about why anyone should consider Crashing Thunder a reliable source of information about his nation or a representative of Native peoples in general. Of course, the book continues to present itself as a mouthpiece for all Native peoples of its era, which is troubling.

Radin did not consult Native American elders, story keepers, writers, or scholars for guidance in creating or appending this book. In the 1920s when it was first published, there were few Native Americans publishing their own writing and fewer still teaching at the college level whom Radin could have consulted. It is unlikely he would have even conceived of doing so considering his own pronouncements of desiring an Indian autobiography and thinking it was culturally appropriate to do one. In addition, he certainly considered himself sufficient for the task of gathering and translating it, so seeking Native guidance was out of the question, even if it had been available. The same is evident for seeking Native Tribal Council approval for its publication.

The 1999 reissue of the text does offer some discussion of the editorial and revision process. This is offered by Arnold Krupat in the foreword and in an appendix. He importantly notes the stylistic and content changes from the original transcript; however, no discussion about cultural appropriateness of the text is mentioned. Indeed, Krupat considers the work an outstanding cultural artifact, rather than a notable text of Native cultural erasure. Claiming that the work is a cultural artifact that expresses cultural erasure, and therefore readers should immediately question its legitimacy would be far more on target. However, simply because a Native person writes about her or his life stories mentioning some Native ceremonies and some part of a Native creation story does not make a biographical text about a Native person worthy, legitimate, or an expression of Native culture.

Crashing Thunder's writing proves repeatedly that readers can get only a glimpse and a shadowy sense of life for the Winnebago at the turn of the last century from his book, which hardly constitutes an important cultural literary transmission.

There is no discussion offered in any edition of the book from contemporary Native American literary critics. An evaluative Native perspective is utterly missing. There is no Native amplification on ceremonies, sacred happenings and stories, or Winnebago and EuroAmerican history. No timelines of historic events or discussion of colonization and its aftermath are included. Only the stories of Crashing Thunder are included; no other members of his community speak or share their experiences. This is an important part of evaluating a work as an Indigenous Communal Narrative, which Radin's book is not. However, the potential for this work to be re-made into a communal narrative is high. Crashing Thunder's writing is filled with detailed stories about his life that include many Winnebago terms, ceremonies, and customs. A contemporary Winnebago elder, scholar, tribal council, and so on could have so much to expand upon to offer a wider audience a significant teaching about their nation. This book has the potential to become very valuable as a Native American auto/biography, if the appropriate persons place it in the proper context. As many Winnebago terms are used, a glossary of terms and their accompanying transliterations and orthography would be possible, useful, and culturally important to include in a future revision.

The creation story of the Winnebagos or of only his clan (so Crashing Thunder claims it to be) appears in the text along with other traditional stories, including a story about Coyote. There is also an origins of the world story later in the book. All the significant players in these stories are men, which is puzzling of course because not only are men not perceived as life bringers on the planet, but a creation story centralizing men is not traditional to Native peoples. The primary mover or god is male as well. To a researcher, this observation must be an immediate red flag denoting a colonized version of a traditional story. Native nations see women as First Beings and Creators; men have no wombs. Radin has no knowledge that either possibility even exists because men are centralized in western culture creation stories so he naturally thought Crashing Thunder's story was merely "natural." Thus, these out of balance traditional stories are not questioned. From what readers learn from Radin's translation, we cannot know if Radin himself changed any parts of it or if the story is considered traditional to the Winnebago people. Answers to both these questions are important.

There is quite a bit of discussion about menstruating women in this text, but no mention of why the menstrual cycle is important, and clearly feared by men in Winnebago customs. In Radin's footnote where he discusses the power of the nation's war bundle he notes without explanation that "women were not allowed to see it or come anywhere near it" (18). Before this observation, Radin comments that the war bundle would kill anything "the only exception being a menstruating woman" (18). Some pages later he adds in another footnote that a menstruating woman could "destroy the power of sacred objects or [men] individuals temporarily sacred" (29). Readers never hear from any Winnebago women or about their traditions, so this cryptic information goes unexplained. In western culture, women's bodily functions were and still are taboo discussions and perceived as dirty. However, this is not at all the case in most Native cultures where women's menstrual cycles were perceived as extremely powerful in positive and awesome ways, and are their direct connection to life and the cycles of life. Women give blood to earth (i.e., life) and men give death blood to earth (i.e., through hunting and warring). Life of course wins over death.

Throughout this book, as noted in *Black Elk Speaks*, Crashing Thunder refers to Winnebago women as virgins and in overall diminishing terms. He tells a story about how he hid a Winnebago woman under a shrub for several days in the rain, and then how he had to return her because he was told she was not good enough for him because she was not a virgin. The story sounds more like what someone would do with a defective piece of mail rather than a human being, and is an utterly non-Native perspective. Here again Radin neither makes mention of nor questions these practices because men treating and conceptualizing women in such terms in western culture's patriarchal social structure is the norm. It is not the norm in Native cultures, however, and mistreating women in most Native nations carried a serious penalty. Further, women were not defined by their sexuality or relationship to men because most Native nations were/are matrilineal.

The theme throughout Crashing Thunder's life story can be summed in a few words: Indian Spiritual Theater, cultural erasure, and drunken debauchery! He repeatedly ends his stories about ceremonies with the lamentation that he does not really care for nor believe in the spirits he was appealing to, but thought only of women and of impressing them. At one point he declares that he lived with as many women as he could because "I had developed the idea that I was a lady-killer" (133). Then he goes on to explain how he enjoyed getting women drunk so he could steal everything they had. Another ruse he would employ was telling people he was a medicine man because he had heard other Indians successfully doing so. This would occur, naturally, when he was drunk.

Another dreadful incident is when Crashing Thunder and some friends murder the owner of some horses, rob him of his possessions, and cut the heart out of the dead man's body because "we had heard hearts were used for medicine" (150)! When recounting the story to his father, Crashing Thunder recalls his father saying, "My son, it is good. Your life is no longer an effeminate one" and then tells him they'll soon have a Victory dance (150). When he went to prison for the murder and learned that his wife had left him, he resolved to "disfigure" her face and give her "a sound beating" (167). When he is released from prison, he is introduced to peyote (a cactus sacred to many Native peoples and used ceremonially) and disparages it at length. After a peyote ceremony, he was told that the Bible condemned having long hair, so he cut his hair and was told that the bad spirits were gone from him now and that Earthmaker "alone is holy" (187). Finding a more colonized procession of events demonstrating utter cultural erasure and internalized self-hatred would be difficult to do. Crashing Thunder concludes his stories by noting chapters from the Bible and speaking in Christian terms as a convert. He disparages the Winnebago people and their customs and exalts Christianity. A pitiful tale, to be sure.

On the last page of Crashing Thunder's testimonial he writes, "I thought I would write down and tell you all these things so that those who came after me would not be deceived" (203). The irony of his statement is bitter: There is little else but deception in this tale if readers expect to learn about Winnebago culture. To use this book as a representation of what happens to colonized people would be more in line with the reality of the stories. Further, the work is not a literary artifact as Arnold Krupat has dubbed it, but is an artifact of colonization and how academia continues to perpetuate colonization by using this and other texts as examples of indigenous culture. It could only be a literary artifact, like the centuries old, Christian church endorsed witch hunt handbook *The Witch's Hammer*, if professors noted that from beginning to end Crashing Thunder's monologue is colonized hot air transcribed by an ethnographer educated on indigenous stereotypes. In other words, naming the collection of stories by Native standards rather than using western culture's labels would reveal that they are not literature or oral keepings at all, but solely represent the exploitation of a culturally broken Native American man for the benefit of a white male academic.

Unfortunately, we still have not arrived at an enlightened point in American institutions of higher learning where books like *Crashing Thunder* would not even be considered for serious literary or cultural studies. Departments of anthropology might successfully use this unaltered book to demonstrate the devastating effects of colonization on indigenous peoples, but it would be better to craft an entirely new text from what bits of legitimate Winnebago culture remain intact in the original manuscript. From this endeavor, with the collective effort of Winnebago elders, tribal councils, scholars, and traditional Keepers, a noble and legitimate literary artifact might be created to the benefit of our national and global communities. Here again collaboration is key and the endeavor to eradicate colonized perspectives from the text is paramount, or at least name them for what they are in a detailed endnotes section. Offering information about Winnebago history during the Indian Removal years that includes maps denoting change of lands and reservation/ incarceration life would be important additions as well. This would give readers a sense of historical context as to why an indigenous man who was born into his traditional culture would eventually come to hate himself, his people, and their ceremonies and become a hopeless drunk. Until Crashing Thunder can be transmitted with appropriate commentary from an editor about the degeneration of its subject, may Radin's work fade into obscurity, where it belongs.

✖ CHAPTER SIX
Tekonwatonti

This chapter illustrates the criteria for authenticating, evaluating, reading, and illuminating a work in the genre of Native American autobiography. Maurice Kenny's work exemplifies the criteria for a work of Indigenous Communal Narrative as previously outlined. It calls the reader's attention to points that distinctly illustrate that new rubric.

Maurice Kenny's poetry collection titled *Tekonwatonti/Molly Brant: Poems of War* was published in 1992 by White Pine Press. He is Mohawk, knows his Mohawk language, and refers to himself as Tekonwatonti's Mohawk poet: the "two Mohawks" (Preface 14). Many of the poems were previously published in both Native American and non-Native literary publications. Of the many advisors who counseled and supported Kenny's work, prominent Native American elder Joseph Bruchac and writer Gerald Vizenor, are included. Kenny describes his work:

> This collection, mainly of personae poems, was composed to shed light on Molly Brant, assure her prominence in the starry firmament, and to right some historical inaccuracies or lies into a semblance of at least poetic truth, if not recorded fact. There has been an attempt at drama, character, and beauty, as well as truth and candor. Many historical and biographical volumes were consulted and some are mentioned in the glossary. (Preface 12)

The work is a communal drawing of Tekonwatonti by the many voices around her and is also an invocation of her own voice: through written history and research, through colonial legend, and through Native oral tradition. This is a biographical portrait that is distinctly Native because it draws from the community for its invention. It values Kenny's relationship with his deceased subject, with his relationship with the land of the Iroquois (his home), and with the spirit of things that are seemingly long gone: All this is woven together so one can know that courageous Mohawk warrior, diplomat, wife, and mother, Tekonwatonti. Kenny uses two essential tools of the Native American autobiographer of deceased Native Americans or historic Native icons: allowance for multiplicity of truths and the significant role of cultural background and Native scholarship of the biographer. To experience what Kenny has created is to experience the Native American way of being—specifically Eastern Woodlands Native culture—that is communal, eternal, socially and politically complex, and alive.

Renowned Mohawk poet and patrilineal descendent of Tekonwatonti, E. Pauline Johnson (1861–1913), used poetry in the traditional way of the Iroquois: to transmit cultural knowledge. Kenny uses the same mode in his work and produces a traditional Honoring Song for Tekonwatonti. Therefore he deepens the authenticity of his work by engaging in practices specific to his Mohawk people to transmit information and culture. An example of an ancient Honoring Song can be found in Mann's *Iroquoian Women* (131). Kenny's work is autobiographical because it is Tekonwatonti's voice that speaks to us from across the ages; it is a communal voice. This is a legitimate and Native-centered way of transmitting life knowledge, history, and communal thinking and ethics.

My intention in this chapter is not to discuss Kenny's work in a traditional (meaning European) literary manner. For example, though I will at times suggest meaning and insight into the poems, I will not analyze or conduct European-style literary criticism or commentary. What I will do is note the points that define Kenny's work as an Indigenous Communal Narrative according to my own rubric: It demonstrates oral tradition, the author has significant familiarity with the subject's culture and history; the work demonstrates communal perspective and Native methodology.

In defining Kenny's work as an authentic Indigenous Communal Narrative, I am differing with the criteria used by Arnold Krupat. Krupat would argue that no auto/biographical work of a deceased Native person can be authentic if it was not tape-recorded; that the subjects of the auto/biographical works are originators; and that gaining the life experiences of one Native person can transmit Native culture. Krupat would not define Kenny's work as a "bicultural composite composition" (or Native American autobiography), as he has described previous biographical work of Natives, because Kenny did not personally interview Tekonwatonti. In addition, despite Kenny's use of poetry written in English, it is far from being "bicultural" as Krupat defined the early European anthropologists' interviews of Native Americans. Kenny is not an outsider as the EuroAmerican autobiographers were, but he is Mohawk-American and is culturally identified. However, Kenny's work is far more accurately and authentically autobiographical than most of the EuroAmerican anthropologists' interviews of Native Americans from European contact through the 1800s.

What makes Kenny's work so is that he already understands his subject's culture and is in fact of the same culture, though it is lived differently from the era in which Tekonwatonti lived. Kenny's position of "cultural privilege" (as scholar bell hooks would describe it) might seem insignificant; however, considering the enormous culture-based communication problems between EuroAmerican culture and Eastern Woodlands Native culture, his position of privilege is quite important. Kenny already understands the cosmology, culture, language, and way of being of his subject, for it is the same as his own. Further, a characteristic of Native culture is to seek out elders and story keepers for the history of the people: Kenny has obviously engaged in this culture-specific task as well. The cultural barriers of communication between Natives and EuroAmericans were significant enough to render most interviews of Natives from European contact through the 1800s generally inauthentic and therefore vehicles for perpetuating negative stereotypes.

By contrast, Kenny's artistic product demonstrates cultural insight, respect, authenticity, and Native methodology which are all hallmarks of superb scholarship and creativity combined. Because he has the privileged position of being Mohawk just as his subject, his work offers significant cultural insight that creates complexity and rich understanding for the reader. This makes his work an emblem of

respect to the Mohawk people, the Iroquois Confederacy, and Tekonwatonti. He creates an authentic work from the stories he weaves
that are based on research of both Native and non-Native sources.
Last, and quite importantly, he uses Native methodology to produce
and present his work which only deepens the reader's experience of
that culture.

Now I will discuss Kenny's work chapter by chapter to demonstrate a Native philosophic method of reading, assessing, and illuminating its authenticity and artistry.

Analysis of Chapter One

Kenny's first and only poem in chapter one is "Te-Non-An-At-Che"
(Mohawk for "river flowing through mountains") which is a creation
story. In the poem he uses the Native tradition of naming found in
many First Nations' cosmologies to create all that would be in the
Haudenosaunee's (Iroquois) world: birds, animals, ritual, life, the
elements, the people, etc. Later in the poem he names the contemporary towns that can be found today in the state of New York (land of
the Haudenosaunee) along with the names of many Native nations.
Although the poem notes the radical changes the Native nations experienced during colonization, the river remains ever present, flowing
through the poem, just as the Native people have remained here in
North America, ever present, life still flowing through them and their
culture. He finishes the poem:

> War
> 　　War
> 　　　　and more War
> 　　　　　　and blood and guts and death
> 　　and the death of
> 　　Indians
> 　　　　the river:
> 　　　　TE-NON-AN-AT-CHE
> 　　　　(River Flowing Through Mountains)
> 　　　　Mohawk
> 　　　　　　drop

drop

drop

To start his work at the beginning—as in the beginning of life and "time"—is to imply two characteristically Native cultural beliefs: that, first, "time" is understood as events which are intertwined, not separated by a notion of "space" which makes events unrelated and disconnected, as western culture perceives it; and, second, that the Haudenosaunee creation story (in essence) at the beginning of his book is essential in telling Tekonwatonti's story because the reader must understand the one in order to understand the other. Wholeness and completion are strived for; to know the woman one must know her people and their way of thinking and being. This is Native methodology in practice. By beginning at his and Tekonwatonti's beginning, he is telling us, "Look at our stars as we (Kenny, Tekonwatonti, the Mohawks, the Haudenosaunee) see them so you can know us. To know life as we know it is the beginning of your knowing Tekonwatonti." How many historic biographies in the western literary tradition begin with a creation story? Imagine the biography of George Washington beginning with the Judeo-Christian story of creation in Genesis. A western reader would have difficulty understanding what one (Washington's life) had to do with the other (Genesis). On the contrary, to a Native reader, Tekonwatonti's life has everything to do with the creation of her people and the land, for they are inseparable and each reflects the needs and life of the other.

Analysis of Chapter Two

In chapter two, Kenny begins to set the events of history, according to the Mohawk. He begins the chapter with a quote from historian Margaret Widdemer from her book *Lady of the Mohawks*: "Among the Iroquois/who hated all whites./Among the whites/who hated all Indians./Hate was in the world/and must be remembered" (27). So the reader moves from the beauty of Haudenosaunee creation in chapter one to the hatred that sprang from the arrival of the Europeans in North America.

The second poem of this chapter is significant and is one of the many poems in the collection which determines the work's authenticity, style of oral tradition, and Native methodology. "Deganawidah: The Peacemaker" is one of the most important figures in Haudenosaunee history as he brought the Iroquois Great Law of Peace to the people. This fact points to a level of cultural understanding and familiarity with Tekonwatonti's people's history that most anthropologists and historians writing Native American autobiography under Krupat's definition missed entirely. This is certainly the case with John Neihardt as he makes no mention of the political structures of the Lakota people in his work *Black Elk Speaks*.

Kenny's poem is written as though Deganawidah is speaking, which begins his style of voice making from his subjects throughout most of his poems. This is a key practice in Indigenous Communal Narrative. The message in the poem is profound: "Ayonwatha/speak my tongue/ embrace my signs and sounds;/ be father of mighty peace/…Your lips are my mouth…" (28). Ayonwatha was the speaker of Deganawidah. Kenny's knowledge of the cultural importance of the relationship between Haudenosaunee councils and their speakers, and the existence of this culturally unique practice, makes explicit his meaningful understanding of Mohawk history and culture. Placing this information so early in the poetry collection continues to lay the groundwork for the reader to understand Eastern Woodlands culture which is essential if one is to understand Tekonwatonti.

So far, we have read nothing of Tekonwatonti nor of her husband, the British Indian Commissioner William Johnson, though the collection is titled with her name. Kenny does not start with her birth, as might be expected from a biographical poetry collection or fiction work in the western literary tradition. Certainly the Native American Autobiographical works characterized as such by Krupat do begin in that exact, western, linear style (information about the subject's birth, linear chronology of events leading up to old age and subject's death). Kenny is telling his readers something far more than the life of Tekonwatonti. His beginning at "the beginning," not her personal beginning, but her people's, demonstrates Native thinking. Her people's beginning, and the earth's beginning, were hers as well. Therein one sees interconnection, rather than division and a sequential chronology, which characterizes a Native cultural point of view.

The poem "New Amsterdam, 1652" is about a starving Native woman who pulls a peach from a Dutch farmer's tree: He shoots her in the head and kills her. This is recorded history, though the Native woman is nameless. Many Native nations consequently burned farms in New York and New Jersey because she was murdered, the poem tells. Why is she included in this story of Tekonwatonti, a westerner might ask? The answers to this question are all Native. First of all, she was a Native woman, a member of one of the Eastern Woodlands nations and therefore valued. Kenny's inclusion of the story of this anonymous Native woman tells the reader that what happened to her matters to her nation and did not happen only to her, *but to her people as well.* She was not without a name to them. Eastern Woodlands people are communal; what happens to individuals has an effect on the entire body of people. Second, the life of a woman was held in high esteem by Eastern Woodlands peoples and the death of a woman required higher restitution to her clan than the death of a man (*Iroquoian Women* 39). Third, Kenny is beginning to weave the history of hostility and blatant disregard of the Native people by the settlers, which is certainly part of Tekonwatonti's history.

Next he writes these titleless facts: "Skanetade (Mohawk)/ Schenectady (Dutch)/ 20 land miles from Albany,/ meant "through the pines,"/ torched and tomahawked in 1690" (32). So not only were the Natives killed, but the land was killed also, and the Mohawk language twisted to fit the newcomers' pronunciation. Again, the westerner might ask of the poet, "why include the deaths of trees in a collection of poetry about Tekonwatonti" and "why note the twisted pronunciation of a Mohawk word?" To the EuroAmerican, these 'things' do not have significant value or consequence and might seem quite out of place in a biographical poetry collection. However, to one who reads with Native cultural understanding, the sheer importance of their placement in the collection is clear. The trees, who were "torched and tomahawked," met the same fate as millions of Native people, that is true, but the trees themselves have value. I refer to them here with the relative pronoun "who" rather than "that" because they are not inanimate, spiritless objects, but important members of Tekonwatonti's community. The trees are merely one part of the whole of life, all of which has value. Their deaths deserve to be included and remembered in the era of Native life and colonial chaos that ensued before Tekonwatonti's birth is what Kenny is demonstrating by including a memorial to them. Further, this information makes clear the type of human beings the European colonizers were: It sheds light on their value system, morals, and spiritual and ethical beliefs. These few lines also signify how colonization permeated every part of Native being and community, which certainly includes the trees who share the earth where the Mohawk lived. With his memorial to them, Kenny is demonstrating that both the deaths of the 'nameless' Native woman who was murdered by the Dutch farmer and the 'nameless' trees who were murdered by the Dutch colonists deserve to be included. All the living beings had importance to the eastern woodlands people in the community of life.

In the remainder of chapter two, Kenny writes of the growing arrogance of the Europeans and their destruction of Native people, language, and land. The Europeans' avarice for land he characterizes in repulsive, lecherous language as a Jesuit priest urges Native laborers to build a fort in the poem "Abbe Francois Picquet": "Blessing squaws on bended knees./   Bringing brats to communion ...Not my purpose./There are enough souls/ in Paradise./My purpose is to construct/A fort...and the Black Robe Jesuits/will dominate/this new world...I pay for blood ..." (38). Kenny is addressing what he clearly, and not alone, sees as the EuroAmerican popular falsehood that all the colonists came to Turtle Island (North America) for religious freedom. Whether or not some or all colonists came seeking religious freedom, lust for land and power were also present to devastating effect. Even most of the 'benevolent' Jesuits were consumed with this brand of avarice. Again, Kenny adds more to the historical landscape, sharpening and focusing the picture before the reader's eyes.

About one-third of the way through the book, Tekonwatonti is at last and abruptly mentioned. A quote from historian James Thomas Flexner's book *Lord of the Mohawks* notes that she was a mighty military commander and diplomat. That is all. She appears on the landscape of her own biography suddenly, as though she had always been there quietly in the shadows, watching; as, perhaps, she was perceived by many European and colonial soldiers and generals whom she destroyed at war. Next the poem "Doug George, Historian" rightly notes, "The pages of our oral chronicles/simmer with voices/and stories of our women./ (Why doesn't the world hear them?)" (50). Then in the next stanzas of the poem Kenny names many Native women from various eras, including Ellen Moves Camp, E. Pauline Johnson, Bea Medicine, Leslie Silko, Grace Black Elk, Wendy Rose, and many more. Why include these contemporary Native women from Native nations across Turtle Island and raise the issue of the absence of Native women's history outside Native communities in a biographical collection? Why does the writer wait until over forty pages into the book to mention his subject? To answer these questions one need look no further than their understanding of the Native point of view. "What is important to whom?" I would ask of my imaginary student of western literary studies.

The first question posed above is about the author's mention of the contemporary Native women. By now, the reader should begin to see the picture Kenny is painting in terms of methodology. His cultural point of view begins to take shape and shine out: The Native women living today are as much a part of the story of Tekonwatonti as she is of their story. This is communal thinking; this is a demonstration of the Native literary and cultural notion Walter Capps names the "perennial reality of the now" (28). Just as Kenny mingles his poems about events from the beginning of life, the 1600s, and contemporary times, so follows his cultural beliefs. The poems mirror his Native point of view and are a model of Native methodology.

The second question mentioned is about Tekonwatonti's absence throughout the first forty pages of her own biography. Without explicitly naming his intention, Kenny discloses his meaning by suddenly including information about Tekonwatonti's adulthood a quarter of the way into his collection. His subject was one member of a nation of people, and what she did was a reflection of them, was done for them, and affected them and all the other lives in her world at that time and now just as they affected her. Indeed, her voice could have been placed nearly anywhere in the volume with equal impact because hers is merely one of the voices of her time, though it is certainly an outstanding one. The question I pose in the voice of the imaginary student about the placement or order of the poetry implies that the reader expects a linear, or western, chronology of events in order to "understand" or experience Tekonwatonti on her or his own terms. To the contrary, Kenny requires the reader to experience Tekonwatonti on Mohawk terms, just as it should be.

The last poem of chapter two is "Beth Brant, 1981: Letter and Post Card." It begins, "There was a dream:/Molly/Joseph./I've lost the language./What does it mean, the dream?/After all these centuries'/travels across northern lands…" (52). In the voice of the ancestor of Tekonwatonti (Molly Brant) and her brother, Joseph Brant, Kenny bares the process of remembering and dreaming one's history. The date is 1981 and Beth, the descendent, begins to consciously swim in her history. The second stanza is:

> I've never given them much thought.
> They've entered and left
> playing such a small role
> in my imaginings,
> but they are my history,
> veins and tongue,
> are cousins, grandparents.
>
> *I believe in dreams.* (52)

As of yet, we have heard nothing from the voice of Tekonwatonti in the collection, yet Kenny writes about her spirit visiting her granddaughter. He tells the reader that she lives and has presence in the now. Before we learn of the details of her life, we learn of her ancestral visitation hundreds of years after her death. There is no time line, and because of that, every moment of the stories in the collection is filled with and fills out all of life. In addition, he notes the role of dreams to Native people in divining, gaining meaningful information, and connecting to the experiences of those who are in the spirit world, another culture-specific characteristic.

Analysis of Chapter Three

Chapter three begins with Tekonwatonti's own creation. "I come from morning with light/I come from the river with song/I come from the marsh with reeds..." (57). The poem finishes with "I go with fire" (57). Within the lines there is inherently far more than the reader might first (or ever) understand, though her birth from the earth and the elements is evident. Her being is filled with the natural world and the other creatures who inhabit that world. It is from these things she gathers her life, and her strength, Kenny suggests or perhaps he merely names what is obvious and true for the Mohawk. The reader does not have to know everything about a poem to appreciate its strength and beauty. If there are cultural secrets in these lines, so be it. I suspect there are profound Mohawk-specific meanings held in the choices he made of plants and animals, but perhaps we do not deserve or need to know specifically of them (their applications in use of medicines or ritual) to appreciate that a deeper meaning exists. Use of plants is often highly guarded knowledge, and perhaps this is why Kenny does not elaborate. (A source for further study is James Herrick's *Iroquois Medical Botany*.) The beauty of the images of the plants builds on the beauty Kenny sees in Tekonwatonti. What the reader does need to recognize in this poem is the connection Tekonwatonti has with the earth; that she is not just from the earth, but is comprised of the elements of the earth, an indigenous belief to be sure.

Next there is a quote from the book *Johnson of the Mohawks* by historian Arthur Pound, which notes that "Nearly every editorial writer, we suspect, has read enough Parkman to glory in his prose and absorb his prejudices" (58). Francis Parkman was an historian of the French and Indian War period, and his work is an American standard (201). Here Kenny allows a contemporary voice to protest the stereotypes wrought by EuroAmericans (Francis Parkman being one of them) about the Native people. In the spirit of the eternal now, he allows the things of the present to speak to the things of the past and consequently rights those wrongs.

This lengthy chapter is filled with historic events and cultural background of the times via the voices of George Croghan, an Irish immigrant second only to William Johnson in his relations with the Eastern Woodlands Native nations (202); Sir William Johnson (also an Irish immigrant and husband of Tekonwatonti); and Aroniateka/Chief Hendrick, the Mohawk Chief who died in 1755 in battle at the age of 70 (202). The second primary theme of the chapter is the passionate love affair between "Molly and Willie" as Kenny often refers to Tekonwatonti and Sir William Johnson. From the poem "Willie to Molly" he writes: "The hair on my legs and thighs/rises/from the heat/of your bricks/between these sheets" (85). There is also discussion in other poems of Tekonwatonti being accused of witchcraft by the German settlers; of Johnson's inexhaustible lust for women, his hundreds of children, and of his forcing himself on and impregnating Tekonwatonti's African slave, Jennie. Rape and excessive reproduction of children were both disgraceful acts to the Iroquois (*Iroquoian Women* 283). Prisoners of war chosen for adoption were completely assimilated into Iroquois culture; this practice was not race based (*Native American Speakers*...49). Perhaps Tekonwatonti wrongly participated in slavery because it was her husband's people's practice and she had assimilated to some degree. Kenny discloses some more of Johnson's character through several poems entitled "William Johnson's Daily Journal":

> ...Washington believes in neither treaty nor gifts nor whatever persuasion. He's a weak commander and greedy. Croghan, slightly more sympathetic, is slightly more lenient with life. He married a Mohawk woman. I fall somewhere between the two, I suppose. I want land as much as they, but am not quite so willing to exterminate a whole people to obtain it....I am an adopted Iroquois, a true Mohawk who not only speaks the language as fluently now as any chief but have half-blood sons by Molly, added protection...If I must bed every Indian woman on this entire continent to satisfy needs, obtain and retain land, then I shall exhaust my flesh on the bed, or on the grass, or in a pigsty...remember I was poor, an Irish lad without holdings, living in the ugliest of poverty...I fear nothing...I do love Molly, but would I allow her to stand in my way? She is the rib of my breast, the Eve of my apple orchard...Her children are my loins and my ashes. (82-3)

In the center of this chapter is a six-page poem entitled "Prayer for Aroniateka/Hendrick," which is the longest in the collection. Kenny notes that the chief was "killed in the battle of Lake George, 1755, his bones were left in the forest" (104). This prayer/poem is based on the Mohawk Condolence prayer, Kenny notes at the poem's end. Here is an excerpt:

> ...We will see the enemy
> Who will see
> Who
>
> Who will watch the hawk
>   ascend
> Who will know the turtle
>   the bear
>   the wolf
>
> Who will feed the turtle
>   the bear
>   the wolf
> Who will watch their house
>   the hawk
> Who will...remember the woman who fell with birds
>   and brought his father and his cousin and his
>   brother...(108)

The singer laments the loss of an elder and with the Chief's passing fears the loss of the Mohawk way of life. As Kenny asks, "who will know and feed and remember" he refers to the Mohawk clans (turtle, bear, wolf) and to their Creator, Sky Woman (the "woman who fell with birds"). However, the poem finishes, "We came in grief and mourning/We/ We will/We will sing/Now" (109). All has not been lost with the loss of Chief Aroniateka, Kenny assures. Though one part of the Mohawk nation has died, the nation continues. Again, Kenny's inclusion of a traditional Mohawk ceremony, and of its message of life and renewal, demonstrates his possessing not only generic information that a researcher might discover, but the more esoteric and rich meaning at the core of the tradition. This is what cultural privilege offers to the wider community or readership of biographical works of Native Americans.

Next, in George Croghan's voice we learn more of Tekonwatonti. In the poem titled by his own name he writes in journal style:

> I talk of possessing Molly. Not possible. Not even Will truly possessed her except on the sheets beneath his fat, and even then I'm inclined to doubt that she did not control. He was sand. She was the most remarkable creature I've ever known. Independent, enigmatic, intricate, unique. While pouring a general's tea she could flash an eye, suggesting that a servant or a half-breed slit his throat, or calmly slit it herself. And on the other hand she could sing the most distraught child into dreams...
>
> They say Will and the English won the war.
> Not true, nary a word of it. Molly, Indian Molly,
> Mohawk Molly, princess and witch, orator
> and advocate, chef and murderess, concubine and mother,
> Molly and the Mohawk men won the war, thinking
> They were winning it for themselves to keep the land...(119)

The chapter ends with Johnson's death and the reading of his will which makes no provisions for Tekonwatonti and their children because Molly and William were not considered legally married by the EuroAmericans. Tekonwatonti's voice is still missing from the book. We hear of her *through* others, especially men, and when she does speak, it is primarily about her love and desire for her husband. "Not much of a biography," my imaginary western literature student exclaims! Indeed, to the western reader the substance of the text is missing, i.e., the subject of the title. However, to the student of Native culture and methodology, it is all too apparent that the voices of the times, the essential community, are who matter. Both the author and the subject are communal people, and reading the poems in this particular order and about many people's experiences surrounding the subject's life is a way of demonstrating what community means.

What appears to be missing from the text are the collective voices of the Mohawk clan mothers. Their voices, as governors and property holders, would be most important both in relation to Tekonwatonti and to the events of her era. It is possible that Kenny intends for them to be the very fiber which holds all the voices together and which do not need to be directly spoken to (which Kenny could not do under Iroquois customs for same-gender communications in council) or heard from. Also, as a male he leaves the telling of these events to the women, which is a gesture of respect. I believe Kenny lets the voice of the clan mothers come through Tekonwatonti, especially through the poems of the earth and other non-human creatures. Often they are the voice of wisdom, as in the poem "Picking Gooseberries" from chapter three of the collection. Still, I must wonder why he does not make an explicit statement from the women's council of Tekonwatonti's era in order to demonstrate the significant role that council played in both the politics of the time and in the Iroquois Confederacy in particular to the most likely uninformed reader. Kenny does offer powerful words from the clan mother Aliquippa later in the collection; they are prophetic and offer a sense of finality. Barbara Mann notes that Aliquippa might well have been the Jigonsaseh (women's title of Head Clan Mother of the League) of her era (*Iroquoian Women* 151). Perhaps he believed the words of one clan mother, speaking for her council and her people, is all that is necessary to demonstrate the centrality of women to the Iroquois. I would suggest more, however. Mann suspects this is Kenny's commentary on western standards that exclude women.

Analysis of Chapter Four

Reviewing the titles of the poems of chapter three, one immediately notices a sharp contrast with those of chapter four. In the previous chapter, the titles are men's names, primarily, and it is through them that the reader begins to know the book's subject, Tekonwatonti. At last in chapter four, she begins to speak for herself. She has grown from young adulthood into a woman; perhaps Kenny suggests that aging is the process by which human beings make a voice for themselves. Nevertheless, his intention on that subject is not important for this work. What is important is that he places the primary poems about the character of his subject at the end of the collection. This is contrary to the western literary tradition that would see its biographical subject as paramount to the text, and place information about that subject foremost in it.

The chapter begins with these titleless seven lines:

> Standing on turtle
> Washington caught
> eagle, braids
> caught the tongue
> roasted flesh
> on his fires.
> The Colonies lit 13 flames. (129)

Herein is the colonial experience of the Eastern Woodlands people that is wrought by their own understanding of the land (turtle), the inhabitants of the land, and the manner by which the colonies lit thirteen flames (by "catching" or possessing or halting the freedom of the inhabitants of the land). Further, it suggests that the thirteen colonies lit their flames by the flesh of the Native Americans. Offering American colonial history from the point of view of the indigenous people is important because those voices are still primarily silent, and the colonizer's experience is the history promoted and the story that is told. On the next page we hear from "Molly":

> May your fire burn
> and allow our fire
> to blaze as well, sign of spirit.
> Symbol of survival,
> our cornfields,
> our white pine of peace,
> eagle diligently watching
>   all the skies.

A people who do not remember: *rain which falls upon a rock.* (130)

Despite the violence between the indigenous nations and the colonizers, Tekonwatonti expresses hope that both the thirteen flames and the fires of the Eastern Woodlands people might burn in peace together. We see her thinking of the entire community of beings in those few lines: still communal focused and desiring life. She is speaking of the Iroquois holocaust of the American Revolutionary War, which is referenced in Mann's *George Washington's War on Native America* (51).

Next there are three short poems which perfectly capture the heart and truth of the EuroAmerican culture and the Native one.

>*George Washington*
>
>"Drive them further
>into the darkest forest
>where not even the French
>can follow with Jesuits
>nor muskets for slaughter."

>*Benjamin Franklin*
>
>"...Exterminate..." (132)

>*Aliquippa*
>
>If only one
>blackberry
>ripens on the bush
>there will be
>sufficient
>seed
>for spring
>brambles. (133)

In George Washington and Benjamin Franklin's poems we hear their own greedy, self-serving desire via the annihilation of the indigenous peoples. They do not wish to be one people with the Natives, share the land so that everyone prospers, and live happily and peacefully together. On the contrary, Washington and Franklin (and the colonists in general) call for the deaths of the original inhabitants so they can have all the land for themselves. Indeed, Mann writes that "land warrants had stood as army pay...usually of 100 acres [per soldier]" (*George Washington's*...147). The land was primarily stolen from the Eastern Woodlands peoples. Washington and Franklin's point of view in the poem support the ethics of western culture that look always toward the self, the "I," and the one. On the extreme opposite end of this philosophy is Native American communal belief. The life of the people, and our connection to all living beings, in this world and the spirit world (as in ancestors), is the heart of life and all socio-political and economic decision-making. Aliquippa's poem, Aliquippa was a principal Clan Mother of the Seneca during this era (Kenny 203), demonstrates this cultural philosophy. Aliquippa's words are recorded; therefore, Kenny has access to them and can weave them in appropriately here. In wisdom she notes that the Native people will continue despite the doctrines and practices of colonizers like George Washington and Benjamin Franklin, even if all but a few Haudenosaunee live, in time, the people will flourish again. Hers is a position of life and regeneration that transcends the treachery and violence of the EuroAmericans. Also, these three poems note differences based in gender between the two cultures: In western culture the men speak solely for the people with little in-put from the women, but in Haudenosaunee culture the women and the men speak for themselves (through their council's speaker) (*Iroquoian Women* 165) and for their people together as one mind (166). This is another cultural characteristic of the Eastern Woodlands people authenticating Kenny's work.

Next are poems of war and of Mohawk rituals leading up to war which include ritually painting a post in the center of the Native town and conducting a specific ceremony around it (Kenny 136). Kenny continues teaching the reader of Mohawk traditions. The poems that follow are in Tekonwatonti's voice and depict her in a way which is startlingly uncharacteristic of how EuroAmerican women are portrayed. Again, there is no mistake that this is a Native woman and that she is perceived not from a EuroAmerican point of view, which would undoubtedly see her as barbaric and unfeminine, but from a Mohawk point of view as a valiant leader and warrior. From "Molly: Passions":..."I loathe war and blood; I think constantly/ of spring, wind rustling in green corn,/violets ripening at the wood's edge,/I hate war, but love this earth and my kin more/than I hate battles and bravery. This/is my passion...to survive with all around me..." (145). The remaining poems from this chapter are filled with war, sorrow, and death. Tekonwatonti occasionally appeals to her deceased husband, William, for guidance and laments his absence.

In the last poem of the collection, also titled "Molly," Tekonwatonti further laments the war along with its eventual bitter loss: "I wish never to live to see/another war./I've gagged on flesh/and choked on blood/...General George, town destroyer,/You have won./Our blood is your breakfast..." (153). In the poem the reader learns of Tekonwatonti's experience in the Revolutionary War, of the losses of the Native people, and of the perverse, sinister legacy George Washington left for all future Americans. A biographer without sufficient Native scholarship, cultural insight, and empathy could not have written this poem. Perhaps only a Native person, or only a member of the Haudenosaunee nation, could have written this poem which contains such heart wrenching loss combined with Eastern Woodlands-centered perspective. This fourth chapter ends in bitterness, but not without first disclosing the significant contributions, hardship, and valiant courage of Tekonwatonti. Chapter four is her war journal, as authentic, gripping, and hard-hitting as any EuroAmerican male general's.

In considering the perceptions of women in the Haudenosaunee culture, it is easy to accept the plethora of poems about both Tekonwatonti's sexuality and warring from chapters three and four. As I discussed earlier, women of the Haudenosaunee held positions of power, respect, and leadership. They had autonomy over their reproduction and their life (*Iroquoian Women* 279). They were diplomats, governors, and warriors (150). To a EuroAmerican biographer not schooled in Iroquoian culture and practicing ethnocentric biases, Tekonwatonti most likely would be perceived as sexually promiscuous, her children illegitimate, and her role in the war would be significantly downplayed. This interpretation is easy to surmise even from today's EuroAmerican beliefs about women, but during Tekonwatonti's era EuroAmerican women had little to zero voice in their society.

In *Born for Liberty*, historian Sara Evans writes about colonial women and specifically notes that, "Colonial courts were filled with cases involving accusations against women ranging from infanticide to adultery, "lewd carriage," heresy, and witchcraft...Puritan ministers railed against the "uncleanness," "whore mongers," and "mothers of bastards" for whom the "fire of lust" led to the "fire of hell"" (31). She makes note that women could serve informally in court as accusers [primarily against other women], "but never judges, lawyers, or prosecutors" (31). From these quotations, the reader should note the condemning connections between colonial women's sexuality, childbearing, and the culture's religious beliefs and how all those notions oppress the women solely. This harkens ever back to western cultural cosmology (the Bible) and the negative perceptions of women that it created and perpetuates. Evans notes that "women knew that they faced death with each birth [and that] ministers reminded them that this was the price for the sin of Eve" (30). Under these cultural beliefs about women, it is easy to understand how there were no EuroAmerican Revolutionary women generals, diplomats, senators, or signers of the Declaration of Independence. This point authenticates Kenny's work, yet again. His work is not Euro-biased nor rendered from EuroAmerican beliefs about women, but is distinctly and appropriately Native. Native women's sexuality and ability to kill and lead armies was not seen as exceptional any more than men's sexuality and ability to kill and lead armies was. These gender beliefs are culture based.

Analysis of Chapter Five

The poems of this chapter are of Tekonwatonti's flight from the new America to Canada and the lamentations for all she left behind. In this first poem she grieves, yet knows she takes everything she loves with her through a bit of Mother Earth in her pouch. The theme of everlasting life continues in the poems that come on the heels of the previous chapter's poem describing her military defeat. The spirit of the Native people is here along with bits of Haudenosaunee history. In the next poem she petitions the English on Carleton Island for a stone house, among other things: "Seed me a pine which will grow/and rise to Sky World/where I will reunite with/the spirits of my ancestors./Seed me another pine under which/the People of the Longhouse/will live in harmony and/happiness/as before and into all futures..." (159). Carleton Island was given to her brother by the British, and this is where he set up the Canadian League. What she desires most of all is the continuation of her nation. Kenny's references to the white pine (Tree of Peace of the League), Sky World, People of the Longhouse, and the theme of the poem are all Native and specific to the Haudenosaunee.

The poem "What the Chroniclers Did Not Record" reviews Tekonwatonti's life in a journal, prose style. It settles the notion, once and for all times, that Tekonwatonti and Sir William Johnson did indeed both have political interests in the other, but they were in love with each other just the same. This poem is evidently speaking back to the pages of EuroAmerican history which cannot conceive of a philandering man and a politically motivated woman simultaneously holding self-serving or nation-centered motivations yet genuinely loving each other. The westerners need to have it "one way or the other," clearly drawn "moral" (according to them) lines which naturally fall much harder upon the heads of their women. Here I refer loosely to Barbara Mann's definition of the EuroAmerican "Metaphor of One" from her book *Native Americans, Archaeologists, and the Mounds* (173). This philosophy would necessitate characterizing Tekonwatonti as either a "bad" woman or a "good" woman. Again to the EuroAmerican, characterizing a woman as politically motivated in love and marriage might lead her to be portrayed historically as either a bad (sexually or politically motivated) woman or a good (chaste or obeying Judeo-Christian laws for married women) woman. Conversely, Tekonwatonti's motivations for her actions in love, sexuality, or politics matter only to the Mohawk in the realm of how those actions affected the Mohawk people. Children belonged to their mother and their mother's clan (*Iroquoian Women* 283), so the matter of Tekonwatonti's children's legitimacy is not an issue, but only a scholar or member of the Haudenosaunee nation would know that and appropriately convey her life to the reader. A EuroAmerican biographer would indeed have difficulty portraying Tekonwatonti as a good Mohawk woman due to the great disparity between the cultural perceptions and societal rules for EuroAmerican and Native women.

Last in this chapter is the poem titled by the location of Tekonwatonti's death, Kinston/Cataraqui Ontario, Canada.

The poem reads:

> A grave.
> Now lost
> in the tangles
> of a growing
> city.
>
> Molly.
>
> Obscured
> by time
> and lack
> of concern. (170)

Analysis of Chapter Six

Kenny rightly observes in the first poem of this chapter the power of Haudenosaunee women and the lineage rights they possess. They keep the lineage wampum, i.e., continuity of life. He suggests that through memory, the realities of truth, power, and nations live, and women are the sources of these things.

> *Women-Memory*
>
> While the men
> were the tongues
> of the Confederacy,
> the women
> were the ears...
>
> Women's hands placed the antlers

of authority
on the leader's head,
and Women's hands lifted them off... (173)

The theme of memory is continued in the second poem, "Call Me...Woman." He writes,

My blood flows through their history...
they cannot deny my place though
my name was cancelled and my flesh left to rot
under the peach tree with the fallen fruit.
Today my blood still flows in the pools
and springs below the cemented earth,
but Van Dyck's peach orchard has long been axed. (174)

Here Kenny refers to the nameless Native woman he wrote about earlier in the collection who was shot by the Dutch settler for eating a peach from his orchard. He most likely also refers to Washington's Sullivan-Clinton campaign of 1779 that destroyed all of Iroquoia's magnificent peach orchards. The Iroquois believe in reincarnation, so perhaps Kenny may be saying this is Tekonwatonti in an earlier life. The poem continues,

My dreams are in the mountains, my dreams
flow in the great rivers, and rise again
and again each spring with the blood-
red strawberries of the meadows... (175)

The poem finishes with "My death cannot be denied, nor my name canceled" (175). Indeed, she lives on in the land, and Van Dyck's orchard is long gone. The murdered Native woman prevailed, and the murderer's legacy has vanished.

The next poem entitled "Aliquippa" is that Seneca Clan Mother's story. She laments her time at war and condemns George Washington for his actions. In her voice, Kenny writes, "...We will have forgotten nothing. Memory/does not die under autumn leaves.../memory is on the wind, the shine of stars..." (179). The poem finishes with a vision:

Twin rainbows will arc the skies,
wild horses prance the clouds.

> Air will clear, eagle take the highest branch
> of the white pine, hawk alight
> on the elm as the river runs swiftly below
> sparkling with speckled trout.
> When darkness calls the fire will cast shadows on cedar
> and the earth shall sing, the earth shall sing.
> I know, I am Aliquippa
>   and I have said this will happen. (180)

Honoring visions and honoring women's words is the essence of this chapter, and is characteristic, a hallmark, of Native Eastern Woodlands culture. Next are two poems in the voice of the famed Mohawk poet, E. Pauline Johnson, who is a great-granddaughter of Tekonwatonti and William Johnson. In the poem she notes how she reconciles her ancestry, "...My mind is fettered with Molly.../Do I stand here in a powdered wig,...What may appear silk is deerskin; these feathers are not ostrich but hawk..." (181). In the poem, Johnson says that a drop of her blood will do away with her link to her grandfather, William. In the second poem, Kenny writes of all that Johnson is..."I am marsh iris, red willow, sumac. I am smoke..." (183). Johnson is a contemporary voice (1861–1913), but still she carries all that Tekonwatonti carried within her over one hundred years before: all the traditions and life of her people and their culture, as women do. The last poem is a recent voice, a Seneca sister-in-law of Tekonwatonti's relative. The poem is filled with musings, rememberings, and beautiful tangents. It is still alive with the connection to the earth and the living. The last lines of this poem and chapter are:

> ...We can walk in the graveyard...show you where Charley
> and my dad are buried under an old cedar tree that sings
> in the wind. The headstones are crumbling. Chicory
> is taking all the vacant lands; ducks come now
> to the creek where beaver used to dam and blue herons
> stalked minnows in the water. (188)

Analysis of the Epilogue

Chief Pontiac of the Ottawa (1720–1769) begins his speech in Kenny's poem with "My footprint is still there" and in another stanza asserts "I am stronger now than ever before/I am many" (191). The last chapter of the collection is a culmination of the voices supposedly of the "past" mingled with the people and things (like water pollution, radiation, beer cans, tires) of contemporary times. The Native people lost the war, were nearly annihilated, and forced from their land and culture, yet they prevail. They have lasted as surely as their culture and the earth have, Kenny boldly states in the first poem of this chapter.

In the poem "There Is a Need to Touch" Kenny argues that he, or Native people in general, need to touch the events of the past through memory in order to connect with them and be reminded of who they are culturally and of their legacy. This is the essential heart of Indigenous Communal Narrative: the power of memory. Within this presumption there is the belief that those things still live; and, indeed, they do. This philosophy is contingent upon a cultural belief system that is communal, that is Haudenosaunee. A communal belief system experiences events, people, stories, and all beings as connected, not isolated and unrelated to each other. He also notes the perverse legacy left by the colonists for all the Americans in one of the few poems in his own voice. Mann notes that "within fifty years, Iroquoia 'would teem with more than a million inhabitants,' EuroAmericans all and [they] were entirely aware of the theft they were perpetrating and even recorded the 'pathos' of plowing up 'charred' corn, mute reminders of Sullivan's destruction" (*George Washington's*...110).

> ...Farmers have turned the earth
> for two centuries. What's left:
> hawks on telephone wires, crows
> laughing, deer bloodying waters,
> raccoons dying in wastes
> of Canajoharie factories,
> fishers gagging on radioactive
> rodents. Molly's bones are in Canada... (193)

The thread of life from Tekonwatonti, even to one of the Haudenosaunee Creators Sky Woman, is evident in the last stanza and circles through Kenny's life. Even in the face of the legacy of the garbage heaps, he plants the white pine and connects with the earth: still living his Mohawk traditions that did not die. The focus is life, not death, and this continues to characterize Kenny's work as Native, earth-centered, and communal.

In "Sitting in the Waters of Grasse River" Kenny regards the birds equally as the tires and trash along the river, and muses about Molly and William's conversation perhaps in that same place with the same types of birds and grasses around them over two hundred years ago. He and his friend Louie have taken their place now, though so much about the river has changed: "...like the Grasse where we now sit,/would be clogged with rubber tires, beer/bottles, discarded trousers, so clogged/no bass can breathe, no turtle spawn/in the wastes and poisons dumped by a thoughtless/society" (194).

The last poem is appropriately about Old Coyote, who lasts and endures, no matter what befalls everything around him, no matter how much the world changes. Coyote is part of the mythos of some Native North American nations west of the Mississippi; he does not appear in Iroquoian mythos. However, in the northeastern United States, coyotes are abundant and Kenny's metaphors from the poem literally apply to the animal. Coyote excels at adapting beyond anyone or anything; his wisdom is to change, grow, and survive. Kenny is telling the reader that this is what the Native people have done also. Like the Native nations after the wars and the slaughter, like Aliquippa's one blackberry, the Native people will go on and on Kenny reassures to the very last. Herein is the heart of Native methodology: the spirit and philosophy of endurance. The last poem of the collection is "Old Coyote in the Adirondacks":

> He stood
> on the shoulder
> of the country road
> waiting
> for us
> to pass

so he could
enter
the night
to sing
on the curve
of his hill. (196)

Conclusion

Kenny's poetry collection about the Mohawk diplomat and warrior Tekonwatonti demonstrates Indigenous Communal Narrative philosophy at its very best. In the work, Kenny gives voice and respect to the culture, stories, and histories of the people surrounding his subject; he does not seek to purport one rigid rendering of the truth about his subject, but he allows Tekonwatonti and the people of her era to speak for themselves and thus includes the reader/audience in the experience.

He uses both the tools of European scholarship (research), his own cultural knowledge, and Native American oral tradition (research) to create his poetry and the collection. Note that traditional styles of western cultural research are simply one way of conducting research and creating scholarship. Gaining access to and studying indigenous oral traditions is another way of conducting research. One is not more valid or accurate than the other. Each merely values and understands human experience and the conceptualization of human experience and history in different ways. Those ways of knowing are born from culture.

Kenny uses the arrangement of the poetry to reflect Eastern Woodlands cultural philosophy of time (events connected) and community rather than the western literary notion that time is linear and events disconnected. He does not focus his work entirely on the subject and therefore creates a reflection of Tekonwatonti's community. Most importantly, the indigenous belief in life, renewal, and survival in the face of great, traumatic events is illustrated in the work. This is a key component of an Indigenous Communal Narrative. Without this explicit message from an auto/biographical text of an indigenous subject, the work would lack cultural authenticity.

In addition to these traits in Kenny's work, he honors elders, spirits, the earth, and ancient stories; accurately portrays his female, Native subject in a way that is in accordance with Haudenosaunee beliefs about women and not a portrayal based in European beliefs about women; and he asked for assistance in and support of his work from Native elders and Native writers. The author succeeds in deeply connecting with his subject so his work is alive and meaningful.

Finally, Kenny's poetry collection corrects EuroAmerican historic inaccuracies and lies about his Native subject that benefits Native nations and the larger American one. This is the ultimate purpose of the Indigenous Communal Narrative: to retrieve what has been lost of indigenous culture and history in mainstream American culture. An Indigenous Communal Narrative should serve to honor past generations and teach future ones about Native Americans. Kenny has created an Honoring Song to Tekonwatonti, a testament to the Mohawk and Iroquoian culture, that conveys an accurate historical record that honors Native oral tradition yet also incorporates European-style learning and research. He has created an example of Indigenous Communal Narrative worth emulating.

❀ WORKS CITED

Primary Sources

Kenny, Maurice. *Tekonwatonti/Molly Brant: Poems of War*. New York: White Pine Press, 1992.

Linderman, Frank B., ed. *Pretty-shield: Medicine Woman of the Crows*. 1932. Lincoln: University of Nebraska Press, 1972.

Miller, Jay, ed. *Mourning Dove: A Salishan Autobiography*. Lincoln: University of Nebraska Press, 1990.

Neihardt, John. *Black Elk Speaks*. 1932. Lincoln: University of Nebraska Press, 1961

Radin, Paul, ed. *Crashing Thunder: The Autobiography of an American Indian*. 1926, 1954. Ann Arbor: University of Michigan Press, 1999.

Secondary Sources

Allen, Paula Gunn. "Kochinnenako in Academe: Three Approaches to Interpreting a Keres Indian Tale." *North Dakota Quarterly* (spring 1985): 84–106.

———. *Pocahontas: Medicine Woman, Spy, Entrepreneur, Diplomat*. New York: Harper, 2003.

———. *The Sacred Hoop: Recovering the Feminine in American Indian Traditions*. Boston: Beacon Press, 1986.

———, ed. *Studies in American Indian Literature: Critical Essays and Course Designs*. New York: Modern Language Association, 1983.

Barron, Patrick. "Maurice Kenny's Tekonwatonti, Molly Brant: Poetic Memory as History." *MELUS*. 25.3/4 (2000): 31–64.

Bataille, Gretchen, and Kathleen Mullen Sands, eds. *American Indian Women Telling Their Lives*. Lincoln: University of Nebraska Press, 1984.

Beauchamp, W. M. "Iroquois Women." *The Journal of American Folklore*. 13 (April-June 1900): 81–91.

Berger Gluck, Sherna, and Daphnew Patai, eds. *Women's Words: The Feminist of Oral History*. New York: Routledge, 1991.

Brinton, Daniel G. *The Myths of the New World: A Treatise on the Symbolism and of the Red Race of American*. 1868. New York: Henry Holt and Company, 1876.

Brodzki, Bella, and Celeste Schenck, eds. *Life Lines: Theorizing Women's Autobiography*. Ithaca: Cornell University Press, 1988.

Bruhns, Karen O., and Karen E. Stothert. *Women in Ancient America*. Norman: University of Oklahoma Press, 1999.

Brumble, H. David, III. *American Indian Autobiography*. Los Angeles: University of California Press, 1988.

——. *An Annotated Bibliography of American Indian and Eskimo Autobiographies*. Lincoln: University of Nebraska Press, 1981.

Capps, Walter, ed. *Seeing with a Native Eye*. New York: Harper and Row, 1976.

Carr, Lucien. "The Social and Political Position of Women among the Huron-Tribes." *Sixteenth Report of the Peabody Museum of American Archaeology and Ethnology*. Cambridge, MA, 1883. 207–323.

Cutter, Martha J. "Zitkala-Sa's Autobiographical Writings: The Problems of a Canonical Search for Language and Identity." *MELUS*, 19.1 (1994, spring) ProQuest Literature Online.

Daly, Mary. *Amazon Grace*. New York: Palgrave Macmillan, 2006.

——. *Gyn/Ecology: The Metaethics of Radical Feminism*. Boston: Beacon Press, 1990.

Deloria, Vine, Jr. *God Is Red*. New York: Grossett and Dunlap, 1994.

——. *Red Earth, White Lies: Native Americans and the Myth of Scientific Fact*. New York: Scribner, 1995.

DeVault, Marjorie L. "Talking Back to Sociology: Distinctive Contributions of Feminist Methodology." *Annual Review of Sociology*, 22 (1996): 29–50.

Du, Shanshan. *"Chopsticks Only Work in Pairs:" Gender Unity and Gender Equality Among the Lahu of Southwest China.* New York: Columbia University Press, 2002.

Evans, Sara M. *Born for Liberty: A History of Women in America.* 2nd ed. New York: Simon & Schuster, 1997.

Fanon, Frantz. *Les damnes de la terre.* 1961. Paris: Francois Maspero, 1982.

Feister, Lois M., and Bonnie Pulis. "Molly Brant: Her Domestic and Political Roles in Eighteenth-Century New York." *Northeastern Indian Lives, 1632–1816,* ed. Robert S. Grumet. Amherst: University of Massachusetts Press, 1996.

Foster, Martha Harroun. "Lost Women of the Matriarch: Iroquois Women in the Historical Literature." *American Indian Culture and Research Journal,* 19.3 (1995): 121–40.

Gilbert, Sandra M., and Susan Guber, eds. *The Norton Anthology of Literature by Women: The Tradition in English.* New York: Norton & Company, 1985.

Grumet, Robert S., ed. *Northeastern Indian Lives, 1632–1816.* Amherst: University of Massachusetts Press, 1996.

Heckewelder, John. *History, Manners, and Customs of the Indian Nations Who Once Inhabited Pennsylvania and the Neighboring States.* The First American Frontier Series. 1820, 1876. Reprint. New York: Arno Press, 1971.

Herrick, James W. *Iroquois Medical Botany.* Ed. Dean R. Snow. Syracuse: Syracuse University Press, 1995.

Holler, Clyde. "Lakota Religion and Tragedy: The Theology of 'Black Elk Speaks.'" *Journal of the American Academy of Religion,* 52 (1984): 19–43.

hooks, bell. *Teaching to Transgress: Education as the Practice of Freedom.* New York: Routledge Press, 1994.

Irving, Washington ["Diedrich Knickerbocker"]. *A History of New York, from the Beginning of the World to the End of the Dutch Dynasty,* eds. Stanley Williams and Tremaine McDowell. 1809. New York: Harcourt, Brace and Company, 1927.

Johansen, Bruce Elliott, and Barbara Alice Mann, eds. *Encyclopedia of the Haudenosaunee (Iroquois Confederacy)*. Westport, CT: Greenwood Press, 2000.

Krupat, Arnold. *For Those Who Come After: A Study of Native American Autobiography*. Berkeley: University of California Press, 1985.

——. *The Turn to the Native: Studies in Criticism and Culture*. Lincoln: University of Nebraska Press, 1996.

——. *The Voice in the Margin: Native American Literature and the Canon*. Berkeley: University of California Press, 1989.

——, ed. *Native American Autobiography: An Anthology*. Madison: University of Wisconsin Press, 1994.

Krupat, Arnold, and Brian Swann, eds. *Here First: Autobiographical Essays by Native American Writers*. New York: Modern Library, 2000.

——. *I Tell You Now: Autobiographical Essays by Native American Writers*. Lincoln: University of Nebraska Press, 1987.

Lerner, Gerda. *The Woman in American History*. Reading, MA: Addison-Wesley Publishing Company, 1971.

Makilam. *The Magical Life of Berber Women in Kabylia*. New York: Peter Lang, in press.

Mann, Barbara Alice. "Euro-forming the Data." In Bruce E. Johansen. *Debating Democracy: Native American Legacy of Freedom*. Santa Fe: Clear Light Publishers, 1998. 160–90.

——. *George Washington's War on Native America*. Westport, CT: Praeger, 2005.

——. *Iroquoian Women: The Gantowisas*. New York: Peter Lang, 2000.

——. *Native Americans, Archaeologists, and the Mounds*. New York: Peter Lang, 2003.

—— ed. *Native American Speakers of the Eastern Woodlands*. Westport, CT: Greenwood Press, 2001.

Mann, Charles C. *1491: New Revelations of the Americas Before Columbus*. New York: Alfred A. Knopf, 2005.

Meyer, Michael, ed. *The Bedford Introduction to Literature*. Boston: Bedford/St. Martin's Press, 1996.

Murray, David. *Forked Tongues: Speech, Writing, and Representation in North American Indian Texts*. Bloomington: Indiana University Press, 1991.

Owens, Louis. *Other Destinies: Understanding the American Indian Novel*. Norman: University of Oklahoma Press, 1992.

Pearce, Roy. *Savagism and Civilization: A Study of the Indian and the American Mind*. Berkeley: University of California Press, 1988.

Perdue, Theda, ed. *Sifters: Native American Women's Lives*. New York: Oxford University Press, 2001.

Powers, William. "When Black Elk Speaks, Everybody Listens." *Religion in Native North America*, ed. Christopher Vecsey. Moscow: University of Idaho Press, 1990. 136–51.

Reinharz, Shulamit. *On Becoming a Social Scientist*. San Francisco: Jossey-Bass, 1979.

Rice, Julian. *Black Elk Speaks: Discerning Its Lakota Purpose*. Albuquerque: University of New Mexico Press, 1991.

Sanday, Peggy Reeves. *Women at the Center: Life in a Modern Matriarchy*. Ithaca: Cornell University Press, 2002.

Sands, Kathleen Mullen. "Collaboration or Colonialism: Text and Process in Native American Women's Autobiographies." *MELUS*, 22.4 (1997, winter): 39–59.

Short, John T. *North Americans of Antiquity*. 3rd ed. 1879. New York: Harper & Brothers Publishers, 1882.

Silvio, Carl. "Black Elk Speaks and Literary Disciplinarity: A Case Study in Canonization." *College Literature*, 26.2 (1999, spring): 137–50.

Smith, J. David. *The Eugenic Assault on America: Scenes in Red, White, and Black*. Fairfax, VA: George Mason University Press, 1993.

Smith, Linda Tuhiwai. *Decolonizing Methodologies: Research and Indigenous People*. New York: Zed Books, 1999.

Spittal, W.G. *Iroquois Women: An Anthology*. Ohsweken, ON: Iroqrafts, 1990.

Swann, Brian, ed. *Coming to Light: Contemporary Translations of Native Literatures of North America*. New York: Random House, 1994.

Udel, Lisa J. "Native American Autobiography." *MELUS*, 22.4 (1997, winter): 175–77.

Vizenor, Gerald. *Narrative Chance: Postmodern Discourse on Native American Indian Literatures*. Albuquerque: University of New Mexico Press, 1989.

Wiget, Andrew. "Truth and the Hopi." *Ethnohistory*, 29 (1982): 181–99.

Wong, Hertha. *Sending My Heart Back Across the Years: Tradition and Innovation in Native American Autobiography*. New York: Oxford University Press, 1992.